The Sw...

written by
Stuart W. Greig

walk conceived by
John Brock

illustrations by
Richard Collier

1st Edition: July 2017, this 2nd Edition: September 2020

Part 1 of the Rivers Trilogy

published by
Pocket Routes
www.pocketroutes.co.uk

ISBN: 978-1788089029

Copyright © 2020 by Stuart W. Greig

All rights reserved. No part of this publication may be reproduced, distributed, or transmitted in any form or by any means, including photocopying, printing, recording, or other electronic or mechanical methods, without the prior written permission of the author, except in the case of brief quotations embodied in critical reviews and certain other non-commercial uses permitted by copyright law. For permission requests, or to enquire about distribution options or reprint fees, contact **stuart@pocketroutes.co.uk**

Front cover:
River Swale at Richmond

Other Titles from the Author

Published by Pocket Routes
www.pocketroutes.co.uk

Herriot Way: A 4-day, 52-mile circular walk around James Herriot country, in the northern Yorkshire Dales
(ISBN: 978-1916117709)

Tributaries Walk: An 8-day, 93-mile circular walk discovering the best rivers, valleys and high paths in the Yorkshire Dales
(ISBN: 978-1916117716)

The other Rivers Trilogy books:

Yoredale Way: A 6-day, 73-mile walk following the Ure, from its source, through Wensleydale to Boroughbridge, near its end
(ISBN: 978-1916117723)

Eden Way: A 6-day, 88-mile walk following the Eden from the Solway to its source, high in the fells of the Yorkshire Dales
(ISBN: 978-1916117730)

Published by Trailblazer Publications
www.trailblazer-guides.com

Pennine Way 2019 (5th Edition): Britain's first National Trail, running for 256 miles from Edale in the Peak District to Kirk Yetholm in the Scottish Borders (ISBN: 978-1912716029)

The Swale Way

DEDICATION

The freedom I have, to walk the hills and valleys of this wonderful country, is only possible through the support of my wife Christine, without whom I would be forever lost.

ACKNOWLEDGEMENTS

Special thanks must go to John Brock, who conceived the walk and whose route I have only been able to improve on, thanks to the introduction of the recent Open Access laws. These have resulted in previously forbidden paths becoming available to responsible walkers.

More recently, valuable works have been undertaken by the Swaledale Outdoor Club and the Boroughbridge Walkers are Welcome committee, on route updates, its signage and on documenting some of the historical interests along the path. I have included these, where relevant.

Additional historical context has been drawn from a most informative book by David Morris, called "The Swale: A History of the Holy River of St Paulinus", ISBN 1850721734, published in 1994 by William Sessions Ltd.

CONTENTS

PART 1 - PLANNING 1
    INTRODUCTION 2
    THE RIVERS TRILOGY 7
    GETTING TO AND FROM 8
    WHEN TO WALK 11
    GENERAL WALKING ADVICE 14
    KIT 20
    ACCOMMODATION 23
    CAMPING 27
    SUPPORT SERVICES 28
    NAVIGATION 32
    THE RIVER SWALE 34
    LEAD MINING IN SWALEDALE 38
    THE SWALEDALE CORPSE ROAD 40
    COMPANION WEBSITE 41
PART 2 - ROUTE DESCRIPTION 42
    SECTION 1 - BOROUGHBRIDGE TO THIRSK 44
    SECTION 2 - THIRSK TO MORTON-ON-SWALE 56
    SECTION 3 - MORTON-ON-SWALE TO RICHMOND 67
    SECTION 4 - RICHMOND TO REETH 80
    SECTION 5 - REETH TO KELD 94
    SECTION 6 - KELD TO KIRKBY STEPHEN 108
PART 3 - THE MAPS 121
    OVERVIEW MAP 122
    NOTES 123

The Swale Way

PART 1 - PLANNING

"It's a beautiful dale, home of the Swale, how well do I love thee, how well do I love thee.
Beautiful dale, home of the Swale, beautiful, beautiful dale."

From the "Song of the Swale" by John Reynoldson

INTRODUCTION

WHAT IS IT?
The Swale Way is a long distance walk that follows the length of the River Swale, from its confluence with the River Ure near Boroughbridge, to its source at the head of Swaledale in the Yorkshire Dales National Park. After visiting the source, the route continues over Nine Standard Rigg to the busy market town of Kirkby Stephen.

Since the beginning of history, explorers have been following rivers, in a search for their source. Although there is no peril involved in the walk to the source of the Swale; no crocodile infested tributaries to cross, no hostile natives or flesh-eating parasites to worry about, there is still magic to be found as we walk upstream.

The Swale Way is a walk of contrasts; along the way it passes through the historic market towns of Boroughbridge, Thirsk and Richmond with their numerous tourist attractions. It visits castles, famous battle sites and historic parkland, wanders through lush meadows and dramatic gorges and travels the length of Swaledale, considered by many to be the most beautiful of all the Yorkshire Dales.

The route was originally conceived by John Brock of the Ramblers Association in 1995. It was then revised to take advantage of the Open Access legislation, by members of the Walkers are Welcome towns of Boroughbridge and Kirkby Stephen. Extensive additional route updates were contributed by Swaledale Outdoor Club, in preparation for the Richmond Walking and Book Festival in 2013.

The guide book draws heavily on all these sources as it traces a path through one of Yorkshire's most iconic landscapes.

HOW HARD IS IT?
Of all the questions addressed in this book, this is probably the most difficult one to answer. The main reason being, of course, is that it is so subjective. This is not going to be an arduous trek for an experienced long distance walker, it will be more like a training walk. For someone who has never

walked for six days in a row, however, this could be a much more serious undertaking. The difficulty will also be relative to how fit you are.

The walk involves a total of approximately 80 miles (129 km) with an overall height gain of around 7,200 feet (2,195 m). The toughest section is the third, between Richmond and Reeth, which includes a lot of ascent and descent across the moorland paths. Although the first section is the longest in terms of length (16 miles, 26 km) it has almost no height gain at all, making it a relatively easy day.

By walking upstream we are basically walking uphill, but the first three days are generally flat and will get your legs warmed up for the sections through the wonderful Yorkshire Dales. Here we get a chance to climb the sides of the valley and look down on the sparkling river below us.

The walk should be well within the capabilities of a regular walker or someone with a good level of fitness. The individual day walks themselves are not too arduous, but the fact that they come one after the other in quick succession does mean you need to be adequately prepared.

The only "disclaimer" contained in this book is here; it is the experience of this author that most people are sensible and have a healthy concern for their own good health and well-being. It is with this knowledge that this book contains none of the usual "take care along the road" type warnings that seem to pepper modern publications. The route description is provided on the understanding that anyone walking along a road, for example, will do so with the degree of caution and awareness that any sensible person would employ. End of disclaimer.

HOW MANY DAYS?
The guide book describes the walk in six sections, each of which can be walked in a single day and each section starts and ends in a village where accommodation is available.

You can, of course, take as long as you like over it and there are many villages along the route (and slightly off it) that can be used to break the walk into smaller, or longer stages.

The itinerary planner below will help you decide where you can stop and how long your stages will be between villages.

ITINERARY PLANNER

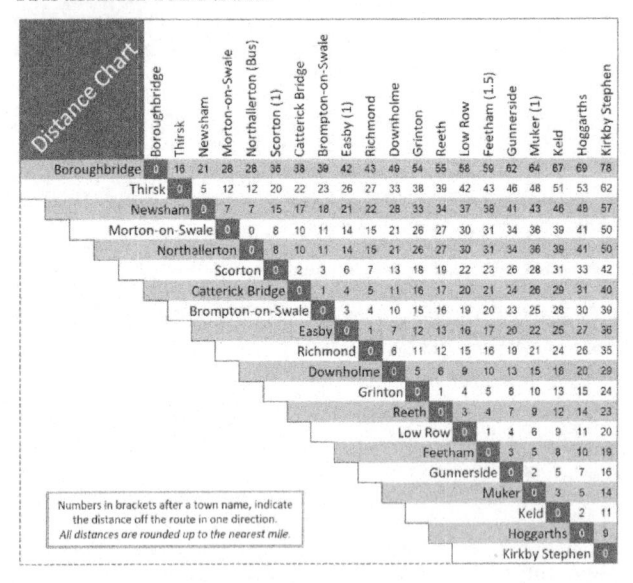

Distance Chart	Boroughbridge	Thirsk	Newsham	Morton-on-Swale	Northallerton (Bus)	Scorton (1)	Catterick Bridge	Brompton-on-Swale	Easby (1)	Richmond	Downholme	Grinton	Reeth	Low Row	Feetham (1.5)	Gunnerside	Muker (1)	Keld	Hoggarths	Kirkby Stephen
Boroughbridge	0	16	21	28	28	38	38	39	42	43	49	54	55	58	59	62	64	67	69	78
Thirsk		0	5	12	12	20	22	23	26	27	33	38	39	42	43	46	48	51	53	62
Newsham			0	7	7	15	17	18	21	22	28	33	34	37	38	41	43	46	48	57
Morton-on-Swale				0	0	8	10	11	14	15	21	26	27	30	31	34	36	39	41	50
Northallerton					0	8	10	11	14	15	21	26	27	30	31	34	36	39	41	50
Scorton						0	2	3	6	7	13	18	19	22	23	26	28	31	33	42
Catterick Bridge							0	1	4	5	11	16	17	20	21	24	26	29	31	40
Brompton-on-Swale								0	3	4	10	15	16	19	20	23	25	28	30	39
Easby									0	1	7	12	13	16	17	20	22	25	27	36
Richmond										0	6	11	12	15	16	19	21	24	26	35
Downholme											0	5	6	9	10	13	15	18	20	29
Grinton												0	1	4	5	8	10	13	15	24
Reeth													0	3	4	7	9	12	14	23
Low Row														0	1	4	6	9	11	20
Feetham															0	3	5	8	10	19
Gunnerside																0	2	5	7	16
Muker																	0	3	5	14
Keld																		0	2	11
Hoggarths																			0	9
Kirkby Stephen																				0

Numbers in brackets after a town name, indicate the distance off the route in one direction.
All distances are rounded up to the nearest mile.

WALK SYNOPSES

SECTION 1: BOROUGHBRIDGE TO THIRSK

Distance: Approx 16 miles (26 km)
Height Gain: 300 ft (90 m)
Walking Time: 6 to 8 hours

Our walk begins beside the River Ure, which we follow until we reach the confluence with the Swale. From here we use riverside paths and quiet lanes to cross the flat expanse of the Vale of York. A lack of suitable footpaths forces us away

4 The Swale Way

from the Swale for a while, so we use a tributary, Cod Beck to continue north. Arable field boundaries, farm tracks and some stretches of tarmac are all employed to deliver us to Thirsk.

SECTION 2: THIRSK TO MORTON-ON-SWALE

Distance:	Approx 12 miles (19 km)
Height Gain:	300 ft (90 m)
Walking Time:	5 to 6½ hours

Today we continue beside the picturesque Cod Beck for a while, through woodland and beside field boundaries, avoiding tarmac as much as possible. We cross parkland and walk through small villages before finally being reunited with the River Swale just outside Maunby. A grassy riverside embankment and quiet farm tracks, offering expansive views, bring us to the village of Morton-on-Swale.

SECTION 3: MORTON-ON-SWALE TO RICHMOND

Distance:	Approx 15 miles (24 km)
Height Gain:	900 ft (275 m)
Walking Time:	6 to 8 hours

A little more up and down than the last two days, today's walk begins to ease us into the hills of tomorrow. Sticking close to the Swale as much as possible, we use field boundaries and riverside paths for most of the day, only resorting to tarmac for a couple of unavoidable sections. We visit the grave of a man reputed to have lived for 169 years and reach the gateway to the Yorkshire Dales, Richmond; with its towering castle and our first waterfalls of the Swale.

SECTION 4: RICHMOND TO REETH

Distance:	Approx 12½ miles (20 km)
Height Gain:	2300 ft (700 m)
Walking Time:	6½ to 8 hours

Today's walk begins beside the Swale with an undulating walk through some lovely woodland, followed by a steep climb, on steps, up to the open moorland on the way into Downholme. Here we can stop for lunch in the Bolton Arms before we head out on one of the finest moorland paths anywhere in the

Dales, around the edge of Stainton Moor. We pass another pub, in Grinton, before our arrival in the busy market town of Reeth.

Section 5: Reeth to Keld

Distance:	Approx 12 miles (19 km)
Height Gain:	1600 ft (488 m)
Walking Time:	5½ to 7½ hours

We're almost close enough to jump into the Swale for the first five miles of today's walk as we leave Reeth via the "Swing Bridge" and follow riverside paths to Low Houses and Isles Bridge. We climb the side of the valley to visit Smarber Chapel before dropping again into Gunnerside in time for lunch. The afternoon sees us hugging the river again using wide pastures and flood plains to reach the dramatic passage through Kisdon Gorge and the gentle climb up to the tiny, time-locked village of Keld.

Section 6: Keld to Kirkby Stephen

Distance:	12½ miles (20 km)
Height Gain:	1800 ft (549 m)
Walking Time:	6 to 8 hours

Leaving Keld we use farm tracks, field paths, old bridges and a short road section to help us achieve our goal of reaching the source of the Swale, in a remote junction of valleys. Another short road section, along the quiet and picturesque B6270, brings us to a moorland path and the long, steady ascent of Nine Standards Rigg, up to the iconic cairns that sit atop it. Here we can soak in the views before beginning the descent into Kirkby Stephen and journey's end.

THE RIVERS TRILOGY

Astride the county boundary between Cumbria, in the west and North Yorkshire, in the east, stands the imposing limestone ridge of Mallerstang Edge. Looking down onto the upper reaches of the idyllic Eden Valley, it is home to the hills of High Seat and the curiously named Gregory Chapel, but more importantly, for us at least, in the space of a kilometre of so, it also gives birth to three great English rivers.

This guide book is the second of three, that describes walks following the lengths of these rivers. Each one can be walked individually, or combined with one of the others to create an extended exploration of these waterways and their valleys.

BOOK ONE: RIVER SWALE

Starting in Boroughbridge in North Yorkshire, the **Swale Way** heads generally north and then east, as it follows the course of the river from its end to its source. The Swale ends as it joins the Ure, from where we walk upstream, through Thirsk and Richmond and into the Yorkshire Dales. Journey's end lies in Kirkby Stephen, in Cumbria. From here we can choose to follow the Ure, back to Boroughbridge, or continue towards the sea, following the Eden.

BOOK TWO: RIVER URE

The **Yoredale Way** begins where the Swale Way ended, in Kirkby Stephen. It climbs up to the Mallerstang ridge, to find the source of the Ure, which it then follows; through the splendour of Wensleydale, the bustling market towns of Masham and Ripon, before arriving in Boroughbridge. When combined with the Swale Way it makes a remarkable circular walk through two of the most famous Yorkshire Dales.

BOOK THREE: RIVER EDEN

The **Eden Way** begins at the coast and the Solway Firth, finding the River Eden as it exits into the sea. It then follows the river through Carlisle and Appleby, beneath the slopes of the Pennine hills, to Kirkby Stephen and then up to the spring which gives it life, on the Mallerstang ridge. Walkers can then continue on, along the Yoredale Way, or follow the Swale Way in reverse, through Swaledale, to Boroughbridge.

GETTING TO AND FROM

Getting to the start of, and returning home from the end of a linear walk can often be the most stressful parts of the planning process. The following information should help you decide on the best approach for this walk.

The first day's walking, from Boroughbridge to Thirsk, is about 16 miles (26km), so consider arriving the day before you plan to start walking. A night in the town will allow for a relaxed start in the morning and a full day to complete the longest section of the Swale Way, not to mention the opportunity to partake in a Full English Breakfast to fuel this long section.

BY TRAIN
Boroughbridge does not have a train station, but train is still probably the most convenient way of getting close to the start point of the Swale Way. York has a main line station and this should be your target. Once at York a frequent bus service runs to Boroughbridge, see below.

Returning from the end of the walk you will be pleased to know that Kirkby Stephen has a train station. Be aware however, that the station is a couple of miles out of town, so make sure you allow plenty of time to get there.

Kirkby Stephen is on the historic Settle to Carlisle railway line, one of the most scenic rail journeys in England. If you're heading south, the line extends beyond Settle to Leeds, giving walkers access to both east coast and west coast services.

BY BUS
If you live in North Yorkshire or the surrounding area then a bus (or two), to Boroughbridge may be possible. In reality, most walkers will use a train to cover the majority of the distance and then bus to finish the journey.

If travelling from York train station, the Number 22 service from York to Harrogate runs every couple of hours from approximately 08:30 to 18:00 Monday to Saturday. A summer bus service, Number 822 covers Sundays and Bank Holidays, but runs less frequently.

If travelling from Harrogate train station to Boroughbridge, the same Number 22 bus service can be used in reverse Monday to Saturday. On Sundays and Bank Holidays the options are much reduced and the Traveline website will provide the most up to date information. **www.traveline.info**

There's hardly any reason to catch a bus from the end of the walk at Kirkby Stephen, the train service provides access to the whole country. However, local bus services can take you to Penrith, Kendal, Sedbergh and Barnard Castle, among other places.

BY CAR
If you're lucky enough to have a lift to the start and a pickup from the end, then your logistical problems are solved. Leaving a car at the start or the end of the walk means you need to rely on the public transport options discussed above to reach the other end.

If you're walking with a friend, or in a group, then leaving a car at each end of the walk will remove any need to rely on public transport.

CAR PARKING
If you're travelling by car, you will need somewhere to park it for the duration of your walk. The first port of call should always be the B&B or Hotel that you use on the first and/or last day of your walk. Many B&Bs will have somewhere for you to leave your car, or know of the best place to leave it within the town such that it causes the least possible inconvenience to residents, or traffic wardens!

The second option will be a public car park, close to your start/finish point. Boroughbridge has a large car park, just off the town centre, in Back Lane. A voluntary donation is requested for the use of the facility.

Kirkby Stephen station has car parking facilities that can be used if you're using the train. At the time of research these were free of charge and there were no time restrictions on their use.

BY TAXI

You may wish to, or possibly need to, use a taxi for the final leg of the journey to Boroughbridge. Public transport may be able to get you most of the way and there are some bus services that will get you all the way, but the closer you get to your destination, the less convenient and regular schedules become.

Always ensure you ride with a licensed taxi driver. The local regulatory authority will require the taxi to display a license plate on the rear of the vehicle and for the driver to display his badge in the cab. All licensed taxis will also have a meter, to ensure a fair and consistent charge for the journey.

Private Hire Vehicles, distinct from taxis, cannot carry passengers unless booked in advance, so you will not be able to pick one up outside a train station for example. PHVs may not have a meter and you should always agree the fare before the journey begins. Feel free to haggle with the operator when you make the booking, but double-check this price with the driver when you meet them.

It's worth remembering that you are unlikely to be able to pay for a rural taxi or PHV with anything other than cash, unless you are paying for a PHV in advance.

A word about website links and URLs

Full addresses for websites mentioned in this book can be found on the publisher's website: **www.pocketroutes.co.uk**

WHEN TO WALK

UK PUBLIC HOLIDAYS
The UK has eight public holidays, also called Bank Holidays. These days fall either on a Monday or a Friday and don't generally occur on a specific date (except Christmas); rather the dates are set by the government two or three years in advance.

Some of the public holidays occur during prime walking months; Easter, early spring and late summer and as a result the availability of accommodation may be restricted on these weekends. Some businesses, banks in particular, will also be closed on these days. Restricted public transport schedules will also be in place. For a full list of dates for this year and the next two years refer to the UK Government website here: **www.gov.uk**

WEATHER
Unfortunately, the UK is not blessed with the sort of climate that allows a walker to say, "I will walk in such-and-such a month to ensure good weather". We are as likely to see glorious sunny days in December as we are in July and similarly snow has been recorded in almost every month of the year in the Yorkshire Dales.

However, as a general rule, the weather is likely to be warmer between May and September than at any other time of the year. Rain, wind, low cloud, mist and fog are year-round occurrences and anyone who has walked in the UK before will be used to this.

A sound philosophy is to "hope for the best and prepare for the worst". This means carrying appropriate cold weather gear such as hats and gloves, especially for the final section over Nine Standards Rigg, which at 2,172 feet (662m) is a proper English mountain and the highest point on the route.

The following climate charts provide a view of the average recorded conditions for the Yorkshire area over the past few years.

DAYLIGHT AND SUNSHINE AVERAGES

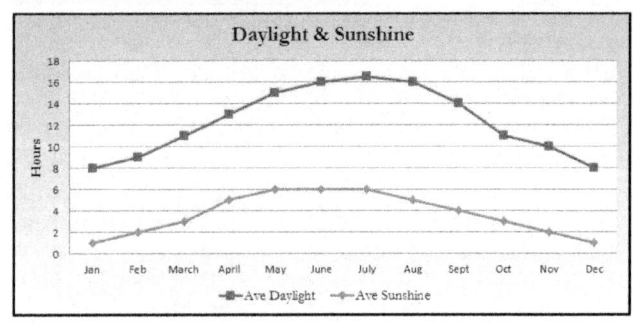

Given the sort of mileages that are involved each day, most walkers should be able to complete the route during daylight hours, except perhaps in the darkest winter months.

TEMPERATURE AVERAGES

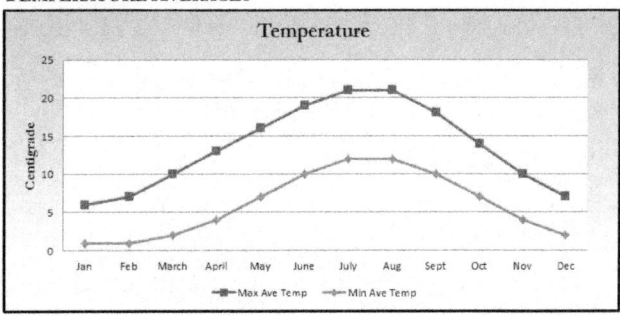

The temperature chart does not take account of any wind-chill that may be experienced, especially on the higher, more exposed parts of the route. In cold and wet conditions, wind-chill can significantly reduce the experienced temperature and even in summer, can contribute to hypothermia.

GROUSE SHOOTING

Some sections of the walk cross the open heather moorlands that now support one of the staple "industries" of the Dales; Grouse Shooting. As you walk along the Swale Way, you will see grouse butts; low stone or wooden structures, normally semi-circular that provide cover for the individual shooters. Many of their walls are topped with heather or turf to help them blend into the surroundings, whether this is to hide their presence from the unsuspecting grouse, or to soften their impact on the environment is unclear.

Some of the roads and tracks you walk along are constructed to support the four-wheel drive vehicles that transport the shooters to the fells.

All this infrastructure supports a four-month grouse shooting season; starting on the "Glorious 12th" of August each year, as parties of shooters, guides, beaters and other support staff head to the moors to shoot the grouse.

If you are walking between 12th August and 10th December, there is a small chance your walk may be delayed or diverted to avoid shooting parties. If you hear shooting close by, keep an eye open for men with red flags, who are there to warn you if you are about to stray too close to a shoot. Do not be turned back, be aware of your rights and make sure you are on the PRoW. The Natural England website (now part of the UK Government website) has more information on PRoW, which can be found here: **www.gov.uk**

FLORA BESIDE THE RIVER SWALE

There are two particularly special times to walk in the Dales; late May/early June and late August/early September. In late spring and early summer, the fields in the valleys will be full of flowering plants and grasses; a veritable explosion of colour all around you with a narrow green path between. These meadows supply the winter feed for the livestock.

In late summer the heather flowers on the moors and the normally brown landscape turns purple for a few short weeks. This is one of the most magical times to walk the high paths in the Dales.

GENERAL WALKING ADVICE

A BEGINNERS' GUIDE

The Swale Way may be the first multi-day walk for many people so this section will cover some advice that will seem quite obvious to experienced long distance walkers, but may still prove useful to beginners.

Footwear: You'll notice the avoidance of the word boot! Boots are not essential for this walk and a comfortable pair of approach shoes, trail shoes or fell running shoes will be adequate. Many people prefer to walk in boots at all times and this is the crux of this piece of advice; walk in what you are most comfortable in. Never use a multi-day walk to try untested shoes or boots. For other kit related advice, see the section on "***Kit***" on page 20.

Maps: There are some sections of this walk where finding the right path or walking in the right direction could be tricky if the mist rolls in or the cloud layer drops. If this happens it's important that you can find your way down off the fells comfortably. Always walk with an Ordnance Survey (or similar) map that covers a wide area around the walk route. The maps provided with this book will lead you along the path, but will not help if you go astray and find yourself walking in uncharted territory. Mark the map with possible "escape" routes; quick exits off the high hills down to a road or village. Don't be afraid to use these routes; it's better to be at the bottom of the hill wishing you were on the top, than on the top wishing you were at the bottom. See the section on "***Navigation***" on page 32.

Compass and GPS: A map will only help so much without a compass or GPS device. Carry one or the other and know how to use it. If you're using a compass, use it regularly; take bearings when you can, especially in mist. If using a GPS check the battery level every morning and make sure you can get a satellite lock before leaving. See the section on "***Navigation***" on page 32.

Weather: The weather on the hills can change quickly, so always try and get a local weather forecast before you leave.

Good B&Bs will be able to provide this or the local Tourist Information Office will also have one posted in clear view. If the weather is likely to be foul and you are not confident in route finding in bad conditions, then consider an alternative low-level route.

Walking Time: Allow plenty of time to get to your destination. An average walking pace is about three miles per hour, but when you factor in lunch and other rest stops, taking photographs, hill ascents, admiring the scenery and all the other little interruptions you will probably not average much more than two miles per hour and often less.

BEING SAFE

Let your B&B owner know where you are heading next and the name of the place you will be staying at. Make sure the owner of the B&B you are heading to knows roughly what sort of time to expect you. If you don't arrive you can expect a responsible landlady to call Mountain Rescue.

WHAT TO DO IN AN EMERGENCY

If you know you're going to be delayed, but it isn't an emergency, for example you've descended into the wrong valley; make sure you inform your accommodation for that evening, or anyone else who may be expecting you. This will hopefully ensure that Mountain (or Fell) Rescue isn't called out unnecessarily.

In the event of an injury to a member of your party try and give the casualty appropriate basic first aid; make sure their breathing is not obstructed, try and staunch any blood flow with items from your first aid kit and keep them warm and dry if at all possible. See the section on "*Kit*" on page 20.

Send for help. If you have a mobile phone signal dial 999 and ask for the Police. Give as many details of your location as you can to the operator, including an OS Grid Reference if possible. If you have no phone signal make your way to a telephone box or the nearest habitation. If you call the Police from a box, stay there; you may need to guide rescuers to the location of the casualty. In most cases the Police will call out the nearest Mountain (or Fell) Rescue Team.

MOUNTAIN RESCUE

The Yorkshire Dales National Park is covered by several mountain rescue teams. For information on their work, fundraising and other activities, visit their websites using the links below:

- Swaledale Mountain Rescue Team
  www.swaledalemrt.org.uk
- Kirkby Stephen Mountain Rescue Team
  www.kirkbystephenmrt.org.uk

DEHYDRATION

The symptoms of dehydration include headaches, muscle cramps, decreased blood pressure and dizziness or fainting when standing up. If left untreated dehydration can result in delirium, poor decision making and possibly unconsciousness.

Dehydration symptoms generally become noticeable after 2% of one's normal water volume has been lost. Initially, one experiences thirst and discomfort, possibly along with loss of appetite. One may also notice decreased urine volume, abnormally dark urine or unexplained tiredness. The simple way to avoid dehydration is to drink regularly and don't wait to feel thirsty, especially in warm weather.

DRINKING FROM STREAMS

As the route is essentially a low-level route and almost completely grazed by sheep and cattle, the wild water sources along the route should not be trusted.

Unless you can find a spring at its source, all water collected on the route should be treated before drinking. The close proximity of villages and towns along the route should enable walkers to collect fresh water regularly.

WALKING WITH A DOG

The Swale Way, along most of its length, uses Public Rights of Way (PRoW), whether they are footpaths or bridleways. On these paths, providing you exercise proper control, there are no restrictions to walking with a dog.

For those sections where the Way crosses Open Access land (see below) and that land is used for grazing sheep or raising grouse then you may be requested to keep your dog under close control and probably on a lead, especially during the period from 1st March to 31st July when animals and birds are raising young.

Although there are no restrictions to walking with your dog, you may find logistical problems along sections of the walk, especially once into Swaledale proper, as many of the stiles are very narrow. Pinch stiles are narrow gaps in the dry stone walls designed to prevent stock moving between fields, without using a gate. As such, large dogs may struggle to fit and you may have to lift them over the wall.

As well as the pinch stiles, there are some gated step stiles through the walls. These are wider but have two or three protruding stones that act as steps on each side, with a spring-loaded gate at the top to protect the gap. These can be awkward to use with a dog.

Pinch stile (left) and gated wall stile (right)

COWS

Sections of this walk, particularly between Boroughbridge and Richmond, will pass through fields containing livestock; some of these will hold cows. In the vast majority of cases they will pay no attention to walkers other than to lift their heads to monitor your progress. Cows, simply due to their size alone, should always be treated with caution however, give them room and avoid coming up from behind and startling them.

Cows with calves should be treated with special care and always try to avoid walking between a cow and her calf, they may see this as a threat. Cows have an instinctive distrust of dogs and may react unpredictably to a dog in their field. Keep your dog under close control, but if cows approach you and become aggressive towards your dog; allow the dog to run free, it will almost certainly be able to outrun an attacking cow and will also divert their interest away from you.

Young cows will often dash across a field to investigate you, but they usually stop a little way off. Resist the urge to run away from an approaching cow or cows. If they approach too close, turn and face them and if necessary wave your hands and shout at them. Make your way to the nearest exit, which may be the way you entered the field and make alternative arrangements to rejoin the path.

You may also encounter bulls in fields with a public footpath, but in general these are no more problematic than cows. A bull with cows is typically quite docile and should present no problem at all. Take more care with a lone bull, however, and give them as wide a berth as possible.

The Ramblers, a UK charity that supports walkers, has specific advice on walking through fields with cows and other animals and this can be found here: **www.ramblers.org.uk**

OPEN ACCESS
Only short sections of the Swale Way rely on the rights granted to walkers under the Countryside and Rights of Way Act 2000, which identified large areas of previously private land and made it "Open Access Land". It also uses Rights of Way that cross Open Access Land, so it's worth being aware of what it is.

This symbol denotes the beginning of Access land and you may see it posted on gates and stiles. A similar sign with a red line through it marks the end of Access land.

Access land, as described in the 2000 Act, includes open country; i.e. mountains, moorland, heath and down, common land and other land dedicated as part of the Act. There are some exceptions to these broad definitions and not all Access land is open at all times. The Natural England website has more information on Open Access, which can be found here: **www.gov.uk**

Walking on Access land can be challenging and dangerous, you will often be a long way from recognised paths or obvious landmarks. Stiles and gates may also be few and far between. As a large percentage of the access land is open moorland, good navigation skills are required.

The latest editions of 1:25k Ordnance Survey maps highlight open access land with a pale yellow shading.

TICKS AND TICK-BORNE DISEASES
The Swale Way route doesn't fall into one of the UK hotspots for ticks, but there's always the chance that you could pick up one of these little parasites whilst walking. There are a number of different tick-borne diseases, but the most common is Lyme Disease (Borreliosis).

It is important to know the best way to remove a tick and therefore the best way to avoid Lyme Disease once you have a tick attached. A specialist tick removal tool is the best implement to use and these can be purchased cheaply from outdoor shops. They weigh next to nothing and are easy to carry "just in case".

More information on how to avoid ticks, how to remove them and the diseases they carry can be found at the British Mountaineering Council website; which is here:
www.thebmc.co.uk

KIT

As this may be the first multi-day walk for some people, the following list includes some guidance on why the items mentioned may be useful. This should not be considered a definitive list; merely a guide to what a walker may want to consider when walking in the hills.

This list is appropriate for someone who is using a baggage courier to move the bulk of their kit; these are the sort of items you may want to carry on a day-to-day basis.

Rucksack: If you are using a baggage courier (see section on "*Support Services*" on page 28) you can get away with a standard day pack, this will probably need to be about 25 litres in capacity. Make sure any pack you buy sits comfortably with items in it; this is worth testing in the shop.

Footwear: You'll notice the avoidance of the word boot! Boots are not essential for this walk, although many people are happy to walk in boots at all times and you should wear what you're most comfortable in. The paths are generally good on the Swale Way and a comfortable pair of approach shoes, trail shoes or fell running shoes should be adequate.

Waterproof Jacket: One of the first items that should go into any pack; the weather in the UK demands that suitable waterproof clothing be carried at all times. When buying a waterproof jacket, consider how packable it is; how much room will it take up in your pack and how much does it weigh?

Waterproof Overtrousers: Almost as important as a waterproof jacket; these will keep your lower body dry and warm. Not as essential in the summer, but an important item for the rest of the year.

Warm Hat & Gloves: Irrespective of what time of the year you are walking, always take some cold weather gear, especially if your route involves a big hill like Nine Standards Rigg (visited on the final section into Kirkby Stephen). The weather on the tops can change quickly. Consider a dry bag for storing the gear, this keeps it dry in the event of rain.

Lunch & Water: If you are walking all day you will need to refuel at some point. If you're venturing high and away from habitation, plan on carrying enough food for an emergency night on the hills. An average day walk of six hours or so is also going to require about 2 litres of water, but take more if the weather is hot and sunny; dehydration is a very real problem.

Survival Shelter: This is really a "nice to have" rather than an essential item. A survival shelter is essentially a large waterproof bag big enough for a couple of people to sit inside knee to knee across from each other. It helps establish a safe temperature environment in really bad conditions, but it's also great for when it's raining at lunch time.

Whistle: A mountain whistle is essential for anyone walking on the hills. It can be used to attract the attention of a rescue team coming to help you, but can also be used to alert other walkers that someone needs assistance. The emergency signal is six blasts on the whistle; repeated every minute. The response is three short blasts. Continue to signal even if you hear the response, it will help guide rescuers to your location.

Head torch: Always useful to have; just in case you ever get delayed and end up walking off the hills after dark. With the advent of LED technology, torches are now very small and very light.

First aid kit: Most supermarket-bought first aid kits will be fine for this purpose. You really need plasters, one or two small bandages, antiseptic wipes and cream and perhaps a sling and some tape. You may wish to add some blister plasters and some painkillers, but it's pointless carrying anything you don't know how to use.

Mobile phone: Although you may not get a signal in the hills, this may still be useful. SMS text messages require significantly less signal than a call, so even when a call is impossible, a text message may still get through. See page 30 for information on mobile emergency roaming.

Sunglasses: Glare causes headaches and can seriously ruin your day, it can be even worse in winter with snow on the ground.

Sunhat & Sun Cream: Think positive!

Waterproof Map Case: This helps keep your map dry and also provides a convenient method for carrying what can be an awkward item, especially if you're using the full OS map.

Compass and/or GPS: It's all very well having the map, but unless you know where you are it's not going to help you very much. The same advice applies to both the compass and the GPS; make sure you know how to use it, before you need to use it.

Kendal Mint Cake: Very few people carry this because they like it, but its weight to calorific value ratio is high and it has a long shelf (or pack) life, so you can leave it in the bottom of your rucksack until the day you actually need it.

ACCOMMODATION

HOSTELS
Due to the closure of many rural hostels, there is only one Youth Hostels Association (YHA) facility serving the Swale Way now, that being at Grinton, outside Reeth. There may be privately run hostels along the Way, some of which may even be located in the old YHA premises.

You no longer have to be a member of the YHA to use their hostels, but non-members pay a temporary membership fee for each night they use a hostel, this is normally about £3.

GRINTON
Address: Grinton Lodge YH, Grinton, DL11 6HS
Tel: 0845 371 9636
Email: grinton@yha.org.uk
Website: **www.yha.org.uk**
OS Grid Ref: SE 047 975
Note: Grinton Lodge is located ½ a mile south of Grinton on the Leyburn road, right beside the Swale Way.

HOTELS & BED AND BREAKFAST (B&B)
The Swale Way is well supported by Bed and Breakfast accommodation, including pubs, inns and hotels and most of it is used to catering to walkers. This may include facilities for drying wet boots and walking gear, and may even extend to the possibility of a laundry service, so be sure to ask.

The list below gives a sample of those available and should not be considered exhaustive by any means. Similarly, inclusion in the list does not signify a recommendation by the author.

BOROUGHBRIDGE
The Grantham Arms
Proprietor: West Park Inns
Address: Milby, Boroughbridge, YO51 9BW
Tel: 01423 323980
Email: info@granthamarms.co.uk
Website: **www.granthamarms.co.uk**
OS Grid Ref: SE 395 671

The Crown Hotel
Proprietor: Best Western Hotels
Address: Horsefair, Boroughbridge, YO51 9LB
Tel: 01423 322328
Email: sales@crownboroughbridge.co.uk
Website: **www.bw-crownboroughbridge.co.uk**
OS Grid Ref: SE 396 669

THIRSK

Fourways Guest House
Proprietor: Mark and Niki
Address: Town End, Thirsk, YO7 1PY
Tel: 01845 522601
Email: info@fourwaysguesthouse.co.uk
Website: **www.fourwaysguesthouse.co.uk**
OS Grid Ref: SE 427 819

Golden Fleece Hotel
Proprietor: Coaching Inn Hotel Group
Address: Market Place, Thirsk, YO7 1LL
Tel: 01845 523108
Email: goldenfleece@innmail.co.uk
Website: **www.goldenfleecehotel.com**
OS Grid Ref: SE 430 820

MORTON-ON-SWALE

Old Royal George
Address: Morton-on-Swale, DL7 9QS
Tel: 01609 780254
Email: theoldroyalgeorge@hotmail.co.uk
Website: **www.theoldroyalgeorge.co.uk**
OS Grid Ref: SE 327 920
Notes: Approx ½ mile from the Swale Way

The Wellington Heifer
Address: Ainderby Steeple, DL7 9PU
Tel: 01609 775718
Website: **thewellingtonheifer.co.uk**
OS Grid Ref: SE 334 920
Notes: Approx 1 mile from the Swale Way

RICHMOND

Pottergate Guest House
Proprietor: Barbara Firby
Address: 4 Pottergate, Richmond, DL10 4AB
Tel: 01748 823826
Email: b.firby4ab@btinternet.com
Website: **www.pottergateguesthouse.co.uk**
OS Grid Ref: NZ 173 012

Cordilleras House B&B
Proprietor: Liz and Gez Cornish
Address: 11 Hurgill Road, Richmond, DL10 4AR
Tel: 01748 824628
Email: cordillerashouse@hotmail.co.uk
Website: **www.cordillerashouse.co.uk**
OS Grid Ref: NZ 169 010

REETH

Cambridge House B&B
Proprietor: Robert & Sheila Mitchell
Address: Arkengarthdale Road, Reeth, DL11 6QX
Tel: 01748 884633
Email: info@cambridgehousereeth.co.uk
Website: **www.cambridgehousereeth.co.uk**
OS Grid Ref: SE 036 998

Kings Arms Hotel
Address: Reeth, North Yorkshire, DL11 6SY
Tel: 01748 884259
Email: kingsarmshotelreeth@gmail.com
Website: **www.thekingsarms.com**
OS Grid Ref: SE 038 993

KELD

Keld Lodge
Proprietor: David Gray & Matt Teague
Address: Keld Lodge, Keld, DL11 6LL
Tel: 01748 886259
Email: info@keldlodge.com
Website: **www.keldlodge.com**
OS Grid Ref: NY 891 009

Butt House B&B

Proprietor:	Jacqui & Chris Giles
Address:	Butt House, Keld, DL11 6LL
Tel:	01748 886374
Email:	info@butthousekeld.co.uk
Website:	**www.butthousekeld.co.uk**
OS Grid Ref:	NY 893 009

KIRKBY STEPHEN

Old Croft House

Proprietor:	Nick and Rachael Godfrey
Address:	Market St, Kirkby Stephen, CA17 4QW
Tel:	01768 371638
Email:	info@theoldcrofthouse.com
Website:	**www.theoldcrofthouse.com**
OS Grid Ref:	NY 775 087

Jolly Farmers

Proprietor:	Carol Pepper
Address:	63 High St, Kirkby Stephen, CA17 4SH
Tel:	01768 371063 / 07854 391384
Email:	enquiries@thejollyfarmers.co.uk
Website:	**www.thejollyfarmers.co.uk**
OS Grid Ref:	NY 773 083

There is also plenty of additional accommodation just off the main route, often within easy walking distance of the path and these may be less busy because of that. You may even be able to arrange a collection from the path for B&Bs that are not close enough to walk to.

If you try and book a B&B and are told it's full; the proprietor will almost certainly be happy to recommend alternative establishments nearby, don't be afraid to ask the question.

CAMPING

CAMPSITES
There are quite a few campsites scattered along the Swale Way route and several more just off the usual route. It is certainly possible to camp the whole route using organised campsites.

Campsites, much more so than B&Bs, come and go frequently, so this guide does not attempt to maintain a list of them. By far and away the best resource for finding information about the nearest campsites, the facilities they have and reviews from campers is the UK Campsite website. You can search by name, location or even view sites on an interactive map. **www.ukcampsite.co.uk**

WILD CAMPING
In England, wild camping is still essentially illegal, without seeking the permission of the landowner first. However, in the hills, farmers tend to accept that wild camping happens on their land. The general rule of thumb should be to camp above the last intake wall, pitch late and depart early and leave no trace of your stay. In most cases, if you abide by these guidelines the farmer will never know you were there.

Large sections of the Swale Way do not lend themselves easily to wild camping following these guidelines. The section between Boroughbridge and Richmond is primarily low level walking through fields and pastures; most of which will be planted, or occupied by sheep or cattle. Some farms may let you camp in the fields, but you should certainly seek approval along this section.

The sections of the walk in the Yorkshire Dales National Park tend to be over higher ground and will provide much better opportunities to wild camp. Even the sections through the valley give easy access to hillsides that can be climbed and suitably isolated pitches found.

SUPPORT SERVICES

BAGGAGE TRANSFER

Over the past few years a small industry has blossomed along the National Trails and Long Distance Paths in the UK; the baggage transfer business. Carrying everything you require for a multi-day walk can be an arduous task and can often be a barrier to some people walking a long distance path. There is now an answer; the baggage couriers.

The baggage courier will collect your bag from the B&B in the morning and move it along the trail to your next stop. Your overnight bag is hand delivered from one door to the other and all you need to carry each day is your normal day-walk pack with its usual essential items.

Some baggage couriers have gone an extra step and now offer package holiday bookings. They will book your accommodation for you and carry your luggage between stops. If you don't have the time or the inclination to contact B&Bs and Hostels to create your own holiday, there are companies out there that will do it all for you. All you need to decide is how many days you want to spend walking the route.

FULL HOLIDAY PACKAGE

These companies will book your accommodation and carry your luggage.

Brigantes Walking Holidays
Tel: 01756 770402
E-mail: support@brigantesenglishwalks.com
Website: **www.brigantesenglishwalks.com**
Note: Baggage Transfer is available separately from Accommodation Booking

BAGGAGE TRANSFER ONLY

Brigantes Walking Holidays
Tel: 01756 770402
E-mail: support@brigantesenglishwalks.com
Website: **www.brigantesenglishwalks.com**

MONEY

The availability of cash along the route beyond Richmond, is not great. The major high street banks have long since abandoned the smaller towns and villages of rural communities. Thankfully some shops now include an ATM (or cash machine) and the towns along the Swale Way that include one of these, are shown below.

Boroughbridge

- Spar - High Street

Thirsk

- HSBC Bank - Market Place
- Barclays Bank - Market Place
- Lloyds Bank - Market Place

Plus others throughout the town

Richmond

- Barclays Bank - Market Place
- Co-op Food - Market Place
- HSBC Bank - Market Place

Kirkby Stephen

- Barclays Bank - Market Street

CASH BACK

One other way to get cash is to buy something with a Debit Card, from which most general stores and supermarkets will provide "cash back". In smaller, rural shops, there may be a minimum spend associated with this service.

TOILETS

The Yorkshire Dales National Park Authority manages a number of public toilets across the National Park, as do local councils and other independent providers along the route. A list of the toilets, both official and unofficial, to be found along the Swale Way is included here.

- Boroughbridge - Back Lane, top end of the town in the car park. Also in Morrisons supermarket at the other end of town
- Thirsk - Marage Road, town centre, outside Millgate car park
- Richmond - Waterfalls car park, Riverside Road, bottom end of the town
- Hudswell Woods - Round Howe car park, over the footbridge
- Grinton - on the B6270, behind the Bridge Inn
- Reeth - north end (top) of the village green
- Keld - on the junction of the two small lanes off the B6270

Remember that all public houses will have toilets, but also be aware that unless you are buying a drink or a meal in the pub, it is good etiquette to ask the landlord if you can use their facilities.

MOBILE PHONES AND TELEPHONE BOXES

Most people carry a mobile phone now. They can be critical when trying to request assistance on the fells, or indeed just for keeping in touch with loved ones back home.

The EE network has the best overall coverage for the Swale Way, with O2 coming a close second. You can pick up an EE SIM card for an unlocked mobile phone from any EE shop. They are normally free if you buy a small amount of credit at the same time. You can also apply online for a SIM using their website.

MOBILE EMERGENCY ROAMING

In October 2009, Ofcom, the UK telephone regulator, finally agreed plans for an emergency mobile roaming service in the UK. This allows a mobile phone to use any available network for emergency calls in the event of no signal being available from the phone's primary network provider. Simply dial 999 or 112 to access the service. You don't need credit on the phone to make an emergency call.

Mobile emergency roaming has its limitations though. You will not be able to receive a call using the service unless you can get a signal from the provider to which your phone is registered, so the emergency services may not be able to call you back for example. The mobile phone also needs to have a registered and activated SIM card in it to use the service.

You can now access 999 services via SMS text message, provided you have registered for the Emergency SMS service. Registration is free, but must be completed before you use the service. See more details here: **www.emergencysms.org.uk**

TELEPHONE BOXES

Many of the towns and villages along the route will include a telephone box among the local amenities, indeed with the closure of so many rural shops and pubs, this is sometimes the only amenity in a village.

In a bid to reduce the amount of maintenance they need and to prevent them being a target for vandals and thieves, some telephone boxes no longer take coins. Instead you will need a credit or debit card to make a call.

Details of how to make calls using a debit or credit card will be included on the notice board within the telephone box.

COVID-19

The devastating economic effects of the Coronavirus pandemic hit the hospitality industry particularly hard. This has resulted in many businesses changing their opening hours, the way they operate and, in some cases, forcing them to close completely.

The services information provided in this guide was correct at the time of publication, but may have changed since. If you hope to take advantage of specific pubs, shops, tea rooms, etc. during your walk, it may be worth checking with them prior to departure.

NAVIGATION

MAPS

The Swale Way requires a number of different Ordnance Survey (OS) maps. The Explorer series of maps are the most detailed maps produced by the OS and have a scale of 10cm to 2.5km, or 1:25,000. Maps with the OL (Outdoor Leisure) prefix, cover the UK National Parks and Areas of Outstanding Natural Beauty (AONBs).

- 299 - Ripon & Boroughbridge
- 302 - Northallerton & Thirsk
- 304 - Darlington & Richmond
- OL30 - Yorkshire Dales - Northern & Central
- OL19 - Howgill Fells and Upper Eden Valley

The OS Landranger series of maps have a scale of 10cm to 5km, or 1:50,000. The lack of detail on these maps will be quite noticeable when you're walking through the valleys, so they are not recommended for this walk. However, the maps you will need are as follows:

- 99 - Northallerton & Ripon
- 92 - Barnard Castle & Richmond
- 98 - Wensleydale & Upper Wharfedale
- 91 - Appleby-in-Westmorland

Maps can be obtained from most high street outdoor shops or online from bookshops such as Amazon. Specialist map retailers may be able to provide them cheaper, so shop around.

The maps provided with this guide will enable you to walk the route, but they do make the assumption that you are sticking to the path described and you don't wander off the map by accident or design. It would be advisable to carry the OS maps in the event that you stray from the described route, or you need to visit places or walk paths outside the scope of this guide.

DIGITAL MAPPING

There are a number of software packages available on the market today that provide Ordnance Survey maps for a PC or mobile phone. The two most well-known are Memory Map (**www.memory-map.co.uk**) for the PC and ViewRanger (**www.viewranger.com**) for mobile devices. Maps are supplied not in traditional paper format, but electronically on USB media or digital download. The maps are then loaded into a dedicated app, normally supplied with the maps, where you can view them, print them and work with them.

The Swale Way walk appears on no maps, not even the OS Explorer range. The walk is not officially recognised and therefore is not included on maps in the same way that the Pennine Way is for instance. With digital mapping you can print a set of maps very easily, that include a highlighted route such as the Swale Way. The whole route is available for download from the companion website and this can be loaded into the digital mapping software of your choice and then printed or loaded into a GPS (see below).

GPS

GPS stands for Global Positioning System and has come to mean a handheld device that receives signals transmitted from orbiting satellites and converts them into a grid reference for your current position. You can upload multiple grid references (or waypoints) to the handheld device and join them together to create a route. When you are out on the hills, the handheld GPS unit will tell you how far and in which direction you need to walk to reach your next waypoint.

The Swale Way is not the sort of walk where a GPS is an essential item of equipment. However, many people use GPS devices as a matter of course when walking and they are certainly an aid to navigation.

The publisher's website for this guide book includes GPS waypoints for the whole of the Swale Way and can be downloaded free: **www.pocketroutes.co.uk**

THE RIVER SWALE

The River Swale derives its name from the Old English word 'suala' meaning swirling or rushing, which bears out its reputation as the fastest-flowing river in England. Inevitably, this means there are lots of waterfalls along its length.

Many of the waterfalls in the Dales are described using the word "Force", as you will see below. This name, like so many in the area, has its roots in Old Norse, the language brought to the area by the invading Norsemen, or Vikings as they have come to be known. The original Norse word was "Foss", which still survives in its own right in some place names, for example the wonderful waterfall of Janet's Foss, outside Malham.

WAIN WATH FORCE
The name, unsurprisingly, also has its origins in Old Norse, "Wath" meaning a ford, and "Wain" meaning a cart - which suggests the place was used as a crossing point, presumably above the falls. Access, even to get a picture, is difficult from the side of the river used by the Swale Way. The best view is from the road, just after the Way joins the B6270.

CURRACK FORCE
The waterfall here is created by Stonesdale Beck, throwing itself over a short series of rocky drops into the Swale. Access is simple, using riverside paths directly from the Swale Way, just before we reach Stonesdale Lane, outside Keld.

CATRAKE FORCE
Catrake Force is a multi-drop waterfall, having four separate steps with an overall drop of around 30 ft (10m). Although impressive, a not inconsiderable effort will be required to access these falls and most visitors settle for a view down onto them, rather than try and scramble down to the river.

EAST GILL FORCE
East Gill Force is a double drop waterfall located just outside Keld, where East Gill drops into the River Swale. The upper section is easily spotted beside the path and the Swale Way passes just to the left of it.

The lower section however, is not so easily seen and a short diversion, along either bank of the Swale, must be taken to get the best view.

East Gill Force, lower section as it falls into the River Swale

KISDON FORCE

Of all the waterfalls on the Swale, this is probably the most impressive and access is relatively easy and well signposted.

Kisdon Force, one of the finest waterfalls on the River Swale

Access to the falls is directly from the Swale Way path, as we climb up to the village of Keld. A finger post points down a steep path and along the river to the falls. After heavy rain the amount of water crashing over the double falls is incredible.

RICHMOND FALLS

The riverbed at Richmond is made up of a series of horizontal limestone slabs, resulting in a series of small waterfalls over a relatively short distance. The falls at Richmond are the last noticeable waterfalls on the Swale, before the river reaches flatter country in the Vale of Mowbray; making them the first that we encounter as we walk upstream.

Richmond Falls, the first waterfalls met on the Swale Way

POOLE'S WASTE

About a mile after leaving Thrintoft (Section Three) we pass an interesting geological feature and a Site of Special Scientific Interest (SSSI). It's well hidden by the tall hedge beside the road and then by an earth bank, but beyond both of these lies an oxbow lake, at Poole's Waste.

An oxbow lake is formed when a meander in a river is cut off and left isolated as the river returns to what used to be its original course. Over time, gradual changes in the course of a river lead to erosion in the outer bank and the build-up of silt on the inner bank. As these processes continue, a meander is formed in the river. The Swale meanders in many places, especially early in our walk and an inspection of the map will reveal potential future oxbows.

The name "oxbow" comes from its distinctive shape, which resembles that of the metal hoop, or "bow" on an ox yoke, used to keep the animal's head in the right place.

KISDON ISLAND

Kisdon is a modest limestone lump, covered in heather and criss-crossed by dry stone walls, sitting beside the Swale, between Muker and Keld. It was formed during the last ice age, around 10-20,000 years ago as glaciers carved out the valleys surrounding it. As the glaciers retreated, the debris left behind blocked the previous course of the Swale, to the south of Kisdon, and found its current course, around the north of the hill. Early maps of the area, dating back to the 18th century refer to the hill as Kisdon Island. Looking at the current OS map, it's easy to understand why.

NEDDY DICK

When we look at the river, we tend to focus on the water, but Neddy Dick looked at the river and saw music. Neddy's real name was Richard Alderson and he was born in 1845, just outside Muker. Many people were known by nicknames at the time, due to so many folk having the same family name and the number of Richard Aldersons was probably confusing.

Neddy became quite a local character, a farmer who was obsessed with music, he collected stones from the Swale and turned them into a lithophone; similar to a xylophone, but made with rocks. He mounted his limestone lithophone on a cart and travelled to local fairs and gatherings playing the strange instrument, no doubt to the astonishment of his audiences. He made other strange instruments too, including a harmonium, a type of reed organ, incorporating more than a dozen bells recovered from old clocks which could be played with a stick. His local celebrity inspired a popular folk song, The Ballad of Neddy Dick, which is still sung today. Sadly, after his death in 1926, his lithophone was abandoned in an outbuilding and eventually the stones were thrown back into the river from where they came.

More information about the man, his life and his instruments can be found on the Swaledale and Arkengarthdale Archaeological Group website: **www.swaag.org**

LEAD MINING IN SWALEDALE

Lead mining in the Dales dates back to Roman times and possibly earlier than that. It was most prevalent however, from around 1800 to the early 1900s at which time cheap imports and increasingly smaller returns finally brought about its demise.

Ore was extracted in one of three ways; either from a shaft, from a level or by hushing. A shaft was a vertical hole dug straight down into a seam, a level was a horizontal shaft dug sideways into the hill and hushing was where water was used to erode the hillside and expose a seam. Many level entrances can still be seen, as can the hushes, but shafts are mostly filled in and covered over with years of growth.

Once the ore was extracted it had to be processed. Often, many teams of miners would be working the same mine and their ore was first stored in a Bouse Team, a series of stone bunkers close to the mine entrance. This kept the ore (or bouse) from different teams separate.

The bouse was then crushed to separate the ore from the rock and then washed to separate more of the waste rock. These processes were often conducted by hand, but in larger operations water-driven ore crushers were built and wooden troughs, called "buddles" were used to wash the ore.

The ore was then smelted in a furnace to produce the metal. Smelt Mills were powered by burning wood, or more commonly peat which was stored in long open-sided, or arched buildings that allowed the peat to dry after it was cut from the surrounding fell. Many peat stores still remain; the arches being a sure sign of the building's use.

As technology developed, the smelting mills were given long flues that stretched up the hillside - sometimes over a mile long - to a huge chimney at the top. As the fumes escaped up the flue they cooled and deposited lead particles on the sides of the flue. Intermittently, boys or small men would be sent up the flue to collect the deposits of lead that had accumulated.

A view of the restored buildings at Grinton Smelt Mill

Finally, the lead was transported to market, along many of the tracks we walk along today. Streams and rivers were forded where possible and packhorse bridges were constructed where fording was impractical. A packhorse bridge has distinctive low parapets (or none at all in some cases), to allow the easy passage of a heavily loaded horse.

A fine example of a packhorse bridge can be seen as we approach Thirsk at the end of Section One. It spans Cod Beck, a tributary of the Swale and is built high above the stream, to allow for a rise in the water level after heavy rains. The Thirsk bridge was built in 1672, with the aid of a grant of £20 and although its primary purpose was for horses, it was heavily used by people too, as it was the only dry crossing of the beck for miles.

Lead Mining in Swaledale 39

THE SWALEDALE CORPSE ROAD

Rural areas all across England will have had Corpse Roads, dating back hundreds of years, and Swaledale is no exception.

A Corpse Road is a path leading from remote rural communities to a church with consecrated ground, in which good Christians could be properly buried. In most cases the deceased would be carried by family members, friends and mourners, often for many miles, in a wicker basket. Only the richest would be able to afford horse and cart to transport the body, the ordinary folk had no such luxury to call on.

As they progressed along the route, the mourners would need to rest, easing the burden from their shoulders while they took their refreshments. In some regularly used places, coffin stones were laid, onto which the coffin could be respectfully placed, protecting it from the damp ground. Often raised off the ground and sometimes shaped exactly like a traditional coffin, many of these stones can still be found, if you know where to look.

Ivelet Bridge, which we meet in Section Five of the Swale Way, between Reeth and Keld, has just such a stone. The graceful, single arched bridge we see today dates back to 1695, but its coffin stone dates much earlier than that. The stone is a Grade II listed structure, as is the bridge itself.

The Swaledale Corpse Road ran from Keld, at the head of the valley, to St. Andrew's church in Grinton. This church, the so-called "Cathedral of the Dales", originates from Norman times and was the only consecrated ground for miles around. Such was their devotion to the church and to the souls of their departed family members, there would have been no question or hesitation in the minds of the living; all the deceased of Swaledale would be brought here.

The coffin bearers of Keld therefore, must have been much relieved by the building of the church to St. Mary the Virgin in Muker, which was consecrated by William Chatterton, Bishop of Chester, in 1580. Their 13-mile journey being significantly reduced in the process.

COMPANION WEBSITE

SWALE WAY WEBSITE
This guide book is supported by a companion website, which can be found at: **www.pocketroutes.co.uk**

The website includes a photo gallery of different places of interest along the Way, as well as many photographs of the path itself.

There is also a Downloads section, where you will find GPS waypoints for the Swale Way. These are free to download and can be imported into many brands of handheld GPS unit.

The website will also be used to identify any errors or amendments to this printed guide, so it may be worth checking this section before you walk.

Every website address and URL used in this guide is also included in the Links section on the Swale Way website. This may make it much easier to access the resources described in this book.

The Swale Way

PART 2 - ROUTE DESCRIPTION

"I gazed at the scene in disbelief. There was everything here; wilderness and solitude breathing from the bare fells, yet a hint of softness where the river wound along the valley floor."

James Herriot's first view of Swaledale

KEY TO VILLAGE SYMBOLS

🏛	Bank/ATM	🅿	Car Park
🛏	B&B/Hotel/Hostel	🍴	Restaurant
🍺	Pub	📞	Phone Box
🚌	Bus Stop	☕	Tea Room
✚	Chemist	🚻	Toilets
ℹ	TIC Office	🛒	Shop
✉	Post Office	🎒	Outdoor Shop
⛺	Campsite		

THE ROUTE

NOTES FROM THE AUTHOR
The notes for the route description are numbered so that you can more easily keep track of where you are on the route, mentally crossing off the numbers as you proceed. Interspersed throughout the narrative you will find 10 digit numbers preceded by two letters; like this (SE 12345 54321). These are Ordnance Survey Grid References and will enable you to check your exact location on the OS map.

I have endeavoured to include every stile, every gate and every turn in the path, but there may be one or two errors along the way. Please feel free to contact me through the website to bring these to my attention and they will be amended for future editions of the guide book.

WALKING TIMES AND DISTANCES
The walking times provided for each section of the walk are estimates only and not based on any scientific formula. Anyone familiar with Naismith's Rule for example, will notice that my estimates assume a much slower walker. Use them as a guide only, your pace will almost certainly be different; such is life.

The simple reason for the difference is that my estimates allow for breaks; quiet moments soaking up a lovely view, pauses for photography, to explore an interesting building, tea breaks, a lunch stop and all the other reasons we decide not to belt along the path at a jog like William W. Naismith obviously did.

Time estimates typically end up being based on my average walking speed of approximately 2 mph, plus a bit of extra time if the section is hilly. Compare that to Naismith's assumption of 3 mph along the flat, plus an extra hour for 2,000 feet of ascent.

The distances for each section and each leg within a section are typically rounded up or down to the nearest ½ mile and the converted kilometres to the nearest integer, which may account for small inaccuracies in the daily mileages. Please forgive me.

SECTION ONE - BOROUGHBRIDGE TO THIRSK
Approx 16 miles (26 km) - 6 to 8 hours

Our walk begins beside the River Ure, which we follow until we reach the confluence with the Swale. From here we use riverside paths and quiet lanes to cross the flat expanse of the Vale of York. A lack of suitable footpaths forces us away from the Swale for a while, so we use a tributary, Cod Beck to continue north. Arable field boundaries, farm tracks and some stretches of tarmac are all employed to deliver us to Thirsk.

BOROUGHBRIDGE

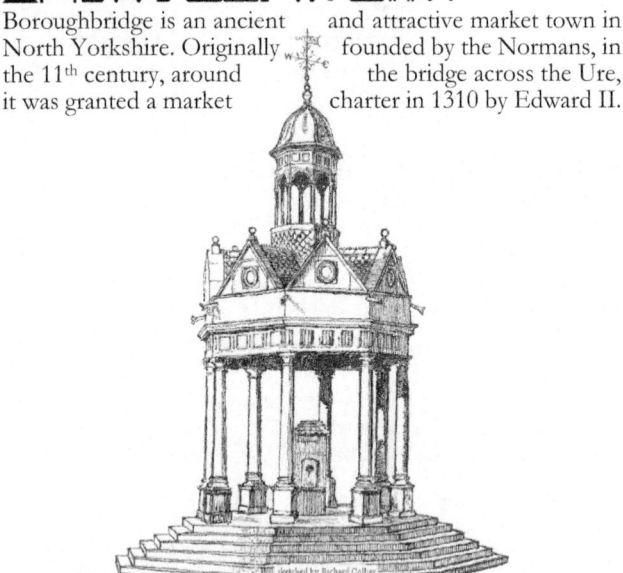

Boroughbridge is an ancient and attractive market town in North Yorkshire. Originally founded by the Normans, in the 11th century, around the bridge across the Ure, it was granted a market charter in 1310 by Edward II.

Boroughbridge Market Cross & pump in St. James Square

This is a great place to spend the night before starting your walk. There's ample accommodation in the **Crown Hotel**, **The Black Bull** and just across the bridge in the **Grantham Arms**.

---

44 The Swale Way

All these places serve food, but there is plenty of other choice around the town if you wish to stretch your legs in the evening.

A **Barclays Bank** is located by the bridge, with an **ATM** (cash machine) should you need it. As you would expect, most establishments accept Debit/Credit cards, but some of the smaller places will have a minimum spend to avoid an additional fee. The town also supports a small **Post Office**, a **pharmacy**, a **Spar supermarket** and there's a **phone box** located in the market square.

There is a **car park** in Back Lane, which works on an honesty box system and here you can also find well-kept **public toilets**.

PART 1 - BOROUGHBRIDGE TO HELPERBY

Approx 6½ miles (10.5 km) - 2½ to 3½ hours

1. We leave Boroughbridge using the wonderfully named street of Horsefair, heading north, past the Crown Hotel on the right and the Post Office on the left. This was once the Great North Road.

2. We soon come to our first bridge of the walk, which crosses the River Ure and was the site of the Battle of Boroughbridge in 1322.

The battle was fought between the rebellious Thomas, Earl of Lancaster and the forces of the English King, Edward II, led by Sir Andrew Harclay. The superior numbers of the King's forces and the experience of their leader made for a short and decisive victory for the crown.

---

3. That wooden bridge (through which a pike was thrust from below to inflict a mortal wound to one of the rebellious captains) has long since been replaced with the stone bridge you see today. Cross the bridge and turn immediately right, between a squeeze point and follow a clear path beside the river.

4. The path is lined by trees and passes beneath Weeping Willows as it hugs the bank of the Ure. After a few hundred yards we reach a lock bridge (SE 40189 67373) and it becomes apparent that we were walking on an island, sandwiched between Milby Cut and the Ure.

5. Use the bridge to cross the lock and turn right on the far bank, following a hedge on our left. When the path bends left, we keep straight ahead, through a metal gate in the hedge ahead of us. Follow the path, beside a wire fence now, on the other side.

6. The path continues between the fence and the river for about 400-500 yards, until the fence gives out and we bend right, around a large tree and into an open field. Keep to the right-hand edge of the field, with the river to our right, screened by tall trees.

7. After another 300 yards or so, we reach the end of the field and a line of smaller trees across our path. Keep right and aim for a kissing gate, hidden beneath a tree in the corner of the field (SE 41018 67341). On the other side, keep to the bank of the river, on the right.

8. The house and farm buildings of Ellenthorpe Hall come into view on our left now and about 200 yards after entering the field we reach a wide gap in the fence across our path. Go through this and follow the thin path that bears left, up into the trees ahead.

9. After just a few yards under the trees the path breaks out into a wide pasture and continues beside the river. Another 150-200 yards and an embankment appears on our left - this was built to prevent the fields being flooded by the river when it rises. The public footpath runs along the top of the bank.

10. The path is easy to follow for the next mile and a half as it sticks close to the Ure, on the raised bank, following the turns of the river through the otherwise flat fields.

11. Soon, another embankment runs in the from the left and the land narrows to a sharp point, where the Ure is joined by the River Swale. Walk out to the metal sign at the point where the Swale terminates (SE 43020 66005) and say hello to the river we will now follow back to its source.

12. Rejoin the embankment, now beside the River Swale and continue along it for another 400 yards or so until we reach a wide metal gate with a wooden stile a few yards to its right. Cross the stile and then through a kissing gate just

beyond it. The path now runs beneath fine old trees and the embankment is not so well defined. The wide field to our left was the site of the Battle of Myton in September 1319.

The Battle of Myton was an engagement in the first Scottish War of Independence. The Scots, aiming to draw English forces away from the siege of Berwick, launched raids into undefended Yorkshire and William Melton, Archbishop of York tried to stop them with a hurriedly gathered force of clergy and local folk. They were easily defeated by the Scots. The number of white-frocked English clergy involved in the battle led to it also being called the White Battle.

13. After about half a mile beneath the trees, we reach an unusual metal pivot gate at Myton Bridge (SE 43597 66772), go through this and turn right, across the bridge.

sketched by Richard Collier

Stapylton Coats of Arms on the supports of Myton Bridge

14. Follow the track, which soon becomes tarmac, into the leafy village of Myton-on-Swale. Other than the telephone box (which now houses a defibrillator machine), there are no amenities for walkers here. The village is mentioned in the Domesday Book as "Mitune" in the Bulford hundred.

Section One - Boroughbridge to Thirsk

The Domesday Book was the inventory of England conducted in the 11th century for William the First, the new King of England, better known as William the Conqueror.

15. At the end of the village the road forks and we keep left, entering the grounds of Myton Hall. We keep to the tarmac lane, passing the hall on the left and the open pasture on the right.

16. Ignore the first left-hand turn, about 100 yards after the hall, instead taking the next left, another 100 yards on, signposted "Helperby 2" (SE 44267 67029).

17. We stay on this very quiet lane for the next mile and a quarter, passing an unusual fence with red-topped, white metal posts and the impressive red brick buildings of Myton Stud Farm before eventually reaching a road junction.

18. Turn left onto this road and follow it for just under a mile, past the imposing boundary wall of Helperby Hall and into the twin village of Helperby Brafferton.

HELPERBY / BRAFFERTON

Helperby is a small village, with very few amenities for a walker. The **Golden Lion pub** serves **food** from midday on Saturday and Sunday, but only after 5pm during the week. The **Oak Tree Inn** in the Brafferton end of the village is open from midday all week and has **rooms** and a **restaurant**. A **bus stop** provides access to services to York and a **telephone box** may be of use to call a taxi, should one be needed.

PART 2 - HELPERBY TO DALTON

Approx 5 miles (8 km) - 2 to 3 hours

1. Continue through the village on the main road, turning left at the top end, onto Bridge Street. As the tarmac runs out, keep left, past an ornate street light and down towards a large tree. Here we pick up a path, at the corner of St. Peter's churchyard, that runs between a wooden fence on the left and a field boundary on the right.

2. Follow this for about 100 yards until we reach a surprisingly impressive footbridge, constructed of iron girders. On the other side of the bridge, take a sharp right (SE 43441 69945), off the more obvious path heading for the tall hedge, and follow a permissive path beside the river.

3. The path uses a low embankment beside the river and after a couple of hundred yards it meets a stone viaduct that used to carry the old Boroughbridge to Pilmore railway. We pass beneath the bridge and continue beyond.

4. The embankment is now mostly disguised by the tall grass, shrubs and wild flowers that grow along it. In the summer these make for an impressive sight. Follow the obvious path for about ¾ of a mile until we reach the road at Thornton Bridge.

5. Turn right onto, and across the bridge. Just before the stone parapet on the left-hand side of the bridge runs out, step over it, onto a thin path through the long grass. A finger post and a notice board for the local angling association identify the route.

6. The embankment on this side of the river is much more overgrown and in the summer the path may be swallowed completely. Use the edge of the field if the overgrowth on the bank becomes too dense.

7. A copse of trees soon appears to our front. According to the OS map, the footpath runs through the wood, but it's much easier to walk along the edge of the field, in front of the wood and meet the tarmac road at a wide gap in a hedge (SE 43697 71675). Turn left along Fawdington Road.

8. Stay on the tarmac lane for about ¾ of a mile, passing the drive to Fawdington House, the red brick building of Fawdington Grange and on to Beck Farm in Fawdington itself.

The sight of the Swale, as we approach Fawdington, is the last one we will have for several miles. We don't meet the river again until the other side of Maunby, tomorrow afternoon. The lack of suitable riverside paths, the desire to avoid as much road walking as possible and the need to find accommodation means that we will have to make do with tributaries of the Swale for a little while.

9. As the buildings of Beck Farm are left behind, the tarmac becomes a gravel track and we bear left at a wide fork, along a track between hedges initially and then with an open field on our left.

Looking across to the right, weather permitting, you may be able to see the Kilburn White Horse, on the wooded slopes of Roulston Scar, about 7 miles away. The hill figure covers about 1.5 acres and is the largest and most northerly in England. The white colouration comes from limestone chippings that have been laid down, rather than the exposure of underlying chalk.

10. About ½ a mile after joining the track, we pass a dense copse of trees at Crow Wood and another 400-500 yards brings us to Mount Bridge and a wide gate over Crakehill Beck (SE 43132 73840).

11. Go through the gate and just beyond, turn right onto another track, with a hedge on our left. A few yards on, go through a wide metal gate and bear left, following the edge of the field, due north, beside a row of wooden power poles.

12. After 300-400 yards a hedge comes in from the left and one appears to our front. The path continues straight ahead, now to the left of the hedge.

If you look to your left, in the distance, you may be able to see a small hill. This is Maiden Bower, all that remains of a castle belonging to the Percy family, Dukes of Northumberland.

13. Keep the hedge on our right for another 400-500 yards until we reach a tarmac lane cutting across our path. Turn right onto this and then almost immediately left, off it, through an unmarked gap in the hedge (SE 43160 74950).

14. Continue ahead, uphill now, with a high hedge on the left and the power lines above. The path takes us over Eldmire Hill and down the other side, where a gap in the hedge allows us into the next field.

15. After following the field edge for 400-500 yards, we enter the outskirts of Dalton and our little track becomes a residential street. After the first house on the left, the road forks and we bear right, downhill gently, past a row of smart bungalows.
16. At the road junction, we find the **Jolly Farmers Inn** (see below). We turn left into the village.

DALTON

Despite its apparent size, Dalton has very little with which to slow us down as we progress towards Thirsk. There's **Ye Jolly Farmers Inn pub**, (open in the evenings only). The only other amenity is the **Post Office**, (closed weekends and Wednesday) which has a small **grocery shop** attached where you can buy something for lunch perhaps. There's a **telephone box**, and a **bus stop** that supports the 60A service to Thirsk, but any other needs will have to wait until we arrive there.

PART 3 - DALTON TO THIRSK

Approx 4½ miles (7.5 km) - 2 to 3 hours

1. After turning left at the Jolly Farmers Inn, follow the road through the village, passing the Post Office and up to the wide road junction, where we bear right.
2. Another 300 yards or so and we turn left at the junction.
3. The Swale Way now follows this road for about 1 mile. It's not a great road for walkers either, with any verges being quite narrow and hedges often tall enough to hide a walker from the sight of oncoming vehicles. Adopt a road position that gives drivers the earliest possible view of you, whilst remaining safe.
4. After passing under the railway bridge at Islebeck Lane and the rather noxious smelling farm at Westholme, look for a track leading into the fields to our left. An ancient and wonderfully camouflaged metal footpath sign points us through the wide gap in the hedge here (SE 44011 77596).

5. Follow the track, with a hedge on its left, until it turns sharp left. The footpath continues straight ahead, across the field.

It has been reported that the farmer may not always clear the right of way across this field as they are supposed to. If the field has been planted and the footpath proves to be impassable, backtrack to the road, turn left along it and use the footpath through Sowerby Parks Farm, which leads to the same footpath we are now aiming for.

6. When crossing the field, if the course of the path isn't obvious, head for the line of trees, to the left of the large barn. The path runs along the front of these trees and then drops between them (SE 43970 77935), just before reaching the buildings.

7. We join a rough vehicle track for a few yards, before taking to the field boundary, climbing gently uphill, with a fence on our left and the open field on our right.

8. At the far end of the field, we continue ahead, passing between tall trees, across a concrete bridge, and follow the field boundary, now with trees on our right. At the end of the next field (SE 43534 78253) we find a marker post with a footpath arrow on it. It points us right.

9. We are now on a grassy track beside the field on our right and an overgrown beck on the left. Follow this for 100-150 yards until we reach an open area between fields. At the time of writing there were four huge drums of cable stored here and a red farm machine, but even if these landmarks don't exist anymore, the transition from green track to rough tarmac should be clue enough.

10. The new tarmac track begins beneath a huge tree and continues with a row of smaller trees on its right, heading for a large electricity pylon.

11. After a couple of hundred yards, the tarmac farm road dog-legs left and then right and passes beneath the power cables supported by the pylon we saw earlier.

12. Don't get too attached to the tarmac though, about 300-350 yards after passing under the power cables, we turn left, off the lane, onto a rough track (SE 44141 78992).

13. The track runs ahead, dead straight, and after 500 yards or so, we pass underneath the power lines again. Shortly after this the track ends at a row of trees, which are lining Cod Beck, a tributary of the Swale. A marker post should be visible, with arrows left and right. We go right.

14. Our path runs between the trees and bushes on our left and an open field on the right. After 150-200 yards, look out for a metal kissing gate on the left. Use this to drop down, through bushes and nettles, into a wide meadow.

15. We get to see Cod Beck now and we follow the path beside the river until we meet a metal kissing gate (SE 43594 79610). This should have our first Swale Way path marker on it!

16. Go through this gate, stick to the path beside the river and 500 yards and four more kissing gates later, we should be deposited into Sowerby Caravan Park.

17. The path keeps to the tall hedge on the left, with the static caravans on the right and after just a few dozen yards we exit by a wooden gate, into an open field. Keep to the left of the field and after 300-400 yards we reach another kissing gate (SE 43619 80322). Turn right through this gate and head under the power lines, following the beck.

18. The path in the field is fairly obvious, and it leads to another kissing gate, that leads out onto a road. Turn right and come to another tarmac lane. Turn left onto this and immediately through a tunnel beneath the A168 road.

On the other side of the A168, look out for the Pack Horse bridge (SE 43537 80660). This was built in 1672 to allow safe passage over the river for pack horses, which were used to carry goods around the country. The arch of the bridge is high enough to allow for rises in the river and the low parapets on the bridge didn't hamper the baskets carried on the backs of the horses.

19. Continue along the road into Sowerby. There's no need to actually walk on the road though, both sides of the street have wide grass verges, as well as pavements.

This is called Front Street and has an avenue of English Lime trees planted to celebrate the Jubilee of Queen Victoria in 1887.

SOWERBY

Sowerby is so close to Thirsk that it's unlikely that any of its facilities will be needed. However, there's the **Crown & Anchor pub** should the need arise and further along the street is **Fantino's bar and restaurant**, which also provides **accommodation**.

20. About ¾ of a mile from the pack horse bridge (SE 42954 81660), look out for a path leading off the road, on the right, with a tall green, metal fence on the right. This cuts a corner and takes us straight into the town.
21. At the end of the path, continue ahead, then follow the road round to the right as it brings us into Thirsk market square and the end of the first day of the Swale Way.

THIRSK

Thirsk is an old-fashioned market town in the Vale of Mowbray (Market Days Monday and Saturday), which is famous for its racecourse. The town is mentioned in the Domesday Book as "Tresche" in the Yarlestre hundred and evidence points to a settlement here as far back as 500BC.

The bustling and often crowded market square has every conceivable convenience the modern-day walker could need at the end of a tiring day. There is plenty of **accommodation**, of all types; B&B, Inn and Hotel. There are several **pubs, cafés and tea rooms**, as well as **high street bank** branches with **ATMs**, a **Post Office**, **Tourist Information** and a **Boots Pharmacy**, you can even get a haircut!

James Herriot (in the form of Alf Wight his creator) had his vet's surgery here, in Kirkgate and the building is now a museum **"The World of James Herriot"**.

Just across the road from the museum is the house where **Thomas Lord**, the father of English cricket and the founder of Lords cricket ground in London, was born.

SECTION TWO - THIRSK TO MORTON-ON-SWALE
Approx 12 miles (19 km) - 5 to 6½ hours

Today we continue beside the picturesque Cod Beck for a while, through woodland and beside field boundaries, avoiding tarmac as much as possible. We cross parkland and walk through small villages before finally being reunited with the River Swale just outside Maunby. A riverside embankment and quiet farm tracks, offering expansive views bring us to the village of Morton-on-Swale.

Part 1 - Thirsk to Maunby

Approx 7½ miles (12 km) - 3 to 3½ hours

1. Leave Thirsk Market Place along Kirkgate via the B1448, past the James Herriot Museum and imposing façade of St Mary's Church. On the opposite side of the road from the church, at the road junction, look for a wide red gate, giving access to the park.

2. A path meanders between the trees, past many benches and a small assault course, until it reaches a bridge over Cod Beck, beside a huge tree stump (SE 42713 82622). Cross the bridge and continue north on the other side, soon crossing a wooden bridge with a Swale Way marker.

Cod Beck extends from above Cod Beck Reservoir at Osmotherley, on the western edge of the North Yorks Moors, through Thirsk and on to join the River Swale at Topcliffe. It has a long history of flooding in Thirsk. The name Cod Beck is a derivative of Cold Beck. The stream runs deep between banks, so is always fairly cool. It is a haven for wildlife and is surrounded by wild flowers.

---

3. A few yards later the path forks beside a black bench, keep left and then through a wooden kissing gate into Centenary Field. The path is quite clear as it crosses the field, heading for a wooden kissing gate, beside a metal gate.

4. Bear right in this next field as the path bends around the trees on our left. At the apex of the bend, ignore the path to the right and bear left, staying close to the beck on our

left. Passing under power lines we soon arrive at a kissing gate beside a bridge over the beck (SE 42544 83217).

5. Go through the gate, but ignore the bridge, instead following the path beside the fence on our left. After a few yards the path heads away from the fence, out into the open field. The path is created by livestock and does not actually match the public footpath across the field.

6. Our path runs slightly right, away from the track, aiming for a stile beneath the trees (SE 42482 83644). However, following the track, brings us to the beck, which we can't cross and naturally directs us to the stile.

7. Cross the stile and bear left, over another stile and into a field. The path cuts the corner of the field, aiming for another stile beneath trees. The path beyond runs between wooden fences. There's a bench here, and you may meet a small herd of alpacas enjoying the shade of the trees.

On our right, hidden by the trees is South Kilvington, which is mentioned in the Domesday Book as "Cheluitun" in the Yarlestre hundred.

South Kilvington church is dedicated to St Wilfrid. It is thought to date from the reign of Henry III. Remains of a Saxon cross in the churchyard indicate that there may have been an even older structure.

---

8. Follow the path as it hugs the beck on our left, beneath Weeping Willows, beside some wonderfully manicured gardens and then through wilder undergrowth. About 500-600 yards after the stile, we reach a wooden footbridge beside a brick wall.

The building to our front used to be a corn mill, the beck was diverted to power the "breastshot" water wheel, housed in the small building on the left. Much of the machinery still survives inside. You can see the water gushing out to rejoin Cod Beck.

---

9. Cross the bridge, go through the gate beyond and follow the clear path as it bends right, passes a tall tree on the left and meets another footbridge partially hidden by trees on our left. Cross this bridge too, through the gate on the

other side and into a field. A Swale Way marker indicates our direction across the field.

sketched by Richard Collier

The water mill at South Kilvington

10. Aim for the small metal gate, set in the wooden fence, beneath tall trees (SE 42277 84244). The little path beyond the gate crosses what used to be a layby on the B1448, but is now overgrown with moss, goes beneath trees and emerges onto the roadside. Cross the road and look for the wooden marker post in a gap in the hedge, beside an old oil tanker.

11. The gap gives on to a field and the path climbs gently up the right side of the field towards the skyline. Here we find a wide metal gate and another Swale Way marker pointing us ahead.

Now that we've gained some height, a look behind will reveal the dark line of the Hambleton Hills, on the western edge of the North Yorks Moors.

12. We are walking beside a tall fence now, separating the path from Underwood Plantation, but a good handrail for the

path. About 350-400 yards along the path, we arrive at a junction, turn right here, keeping the field boundary hedge on our right.

13. We pass a bench, dedicated to "Barnaby" with a view across to the hills above Wensleydale and Nidderdale. Follow the hedge for about 600 yards, to the end of the field, where we meet a new line of bushes to our front (SE 41428 84623). The path bends left here in front of the new hedge.

14. At the bottom of the field, turn right beside a pair of hawthorn bushes, keeping to the right-hand edge of the new field. The public footpath through this field cuts the corners, but if the field has been planted with a crop, the line of the path is unlikely to have been cleared, so stick to the field margin. On a clear day, the views to the west, towards the Yorkshire Dales are impressive.

15. About 150 yards after entering the field, keep an eye out, in the hedge on our right, for an unusual statue (SE 41113 84805). What appears to be a Buddhist Teppanom statue has been placed beside the path, for reasons unknown.

16. Almost exactly ½ a mile into the field, the path heads into the undergrowth on the right, marked by a knee-high sign. It can be easy to miss in the height of summer, especially as the path also appears to continue along the side of the field. In the dappled sunlight beneath the canopy, bluebells abound in May and the path is much clearer.

17. Follow it past a footpath marker post, to a wooden fence, where we keep right and squeeze between the fence and the undergrowth of Big Wood. Towards the end of the fence we pass through a kissing gate, then out into a wide park. Continue with the edge of the wood on our right until that gives out, then keep straight ahead until we meet the tarmac drive of Thornton Stud (SE 40215 85460).

Thornton Stud has a landscape park with belts, lodges and a drive system. These features are associated with the stud farm and the now demolished country house. Thornton was first created between 1660 and 1680. The stud was founded in 1918 and the hall was demolished shortly afterwards. During the

20th century it was owned by three of the most successful owner-breeders in the country and was home to a Yorkshire-based champion sire.

18. Turn left onto the drive and follow it through the park. After 500-600 yards we go through a gate beside a cattle grid and enter the trees, still on tarmac. A little further on, a blue Swale Way marker points us left at a fork in the road, beyond which we pass through a gateway.

sketched by Richard Collier

The gates of Thornton Stud

19. Another 600 yards or so along the tarmac and we arrive at the hugely impressive gates of Thornton Stud (SE 39339 84513). Go through these and turn right along the road and over the railway bridge. About 100 yards beyond the bridge, look out for a farm entrance on the right. This is Willow Bridge Farm, a new addition built a few years ago and only appears on the most recent OS maps.

Despite access reports being filed by the author and by others, the path through the farm can still be difficult, and the public right of way is not obvious. After a recent discussion with the landowner this will hopefully be resolved in the near future. The following two points may change as access improves.

20. If the wide gate from the road is locked, use the gate and stile in the fence to its right to enter the farmyard. Look for two metal gates, side-by-side on the right and use the left-hand gate to enter a paddock. Turn left along a clear path and aim for the right-hand edge of the line of bushes ahead.

21. Here we find a makeshift bridge that has been provided by the landowner to cross the ditch. Bear left over the bridge, aiming for the tall fir trees and for the stile at their base (SE 38861 84620).

22. Push through the small plantation and out into the field beyond. Keep the hedgerow to our right as we continue.

23. After about 250 yards we reach a break between the fields and a rough track across our path, turn left onto this track. Follow it for about 500 yards and at the beginning of the 3rd field on our left, look for a well disguised and unmarked gap in the hedge on our right. Go through this, down to a ditch and over a small bridge and stile, into the next field.

24. Head half left across this field, aiming half way between the green roofed building on the right and the grey sided building on the left. After 300 yards we find a gate and a rather awkward stile beneath a tree (SE 38004 84746), either of which give out on to a lane.

25. Turn right along the lane, passing the **Newsham Grange B&B** (Tel: 01845 588047) on the left and just beyond it, turn left, along the lane signposted "Kirby Wiske ¼ & Maunby 2".

26. Follow the lane, which has unusual raised pavements for some of its length, for about 400 yards, into the tiny village of Kirby Wiske.

KIRBY WISKE

🛏 **P** ((•))

Kirby Wiske is mentioned in the Domesday Book as "Kirkebi", in the Allerton hundred. There may well have been reason to record the place at the time, but no longer. There is a B&B, on the main road, before you enter the village, **Newsham Grange Farm**, but other than a tiny **car park** and **telephone box** there is nothing else to delay us here. The parish church of St. John the Baptist, originally built in the 12th century, is an impressive building for such a small settlement.

Roger Ascham, Queen Elizabeth I's tutor was born in Kirby Wiske in 1515.

---

27. Walk past the church on the right, the village hall on the left and take the left turn into Green Lane, signposted "No Through Road".

28. The lane passes Sion Hill, with its Bird of Prey Centre and continues, for about 400-450 yards to meet a finger post with a Swale Way marker (SE 37178 84847), pointing us straight ahead, while the lane turns left.

29. The tarmac soon becomes gravel and the views to our left and right become expansive, out across the fields. About 500 yards after the finger post, the track bends left, through the hedge and another 500 yards up to the buildings of Kirby Grange.

30. Keep the buildings to the right and leave the track, continuing straight ahead, now on a grassy path with a hedge on our right. At the top of the field, turn right, keeping beside the hedge.

31. After just a few yards the hedge ends (SE 36238 85054) and the path continues straight across the next field. This farmer seems to be better at marking his footpaths and even with a tall crop in the field, at the time of writing, the path was wide and obvious.

32. Cross the field to a stile and beyond that, aim for the right-hand end of the hedge across our path. Here we cross a farm track and use another stile to enter another field.

33. Still continuing straight ahead, cross the field, drop down into the next field, and at the far side we find a tiny wooden bridge and a stile with a Swale Way marker (SE 35831 85545).

34. Keep to the hedge on the right until we reach a wide gap into the next field. Head half left across this field. We're aiming for a broken post with a right turn arrow on it, positioned at the left-hand end of the hedge that comes in from our right, where it meets a tall tree. Follow the arrow and turn right, keeping to the field boundary.

35. We soon reach another stile through a tall hedge, beyond which we keep to the hedge on our right. After about 400-450 yards we reach a red metal gate (SE 35319 85893), with a stile beside it, that takes us into a wide pasture.

36. Bear slightly right across the pasture, aiming for the wooden fence at the foot of a line of tall trees ahead of us. The more obvious footpath into Maunby, as shown on the OS map, is blocked, so when we reach the wooden fence, turn right along its face until we find a wooden gate beneath the trees.

37. Go through this, along the wide path through the trees to another wooden gate. The path takes us past a red brick building and soon arrives at a metal gate in a wooden fence (SE 35293 86379). Go through the field beyond, keeping to the fence on the left, to reach a small gate beneath the trees.

38. The gate gives on to the yard of an old chapel. Walk around the side of the little church, through its gate and onto the lane in Maunby. Turn left along the lane into the village.

Maunby

Maunby has very little to interest us, unless you time your arrival carefully, to coincide with the opening times of the excellent public house. The **Buck Inn** serves **food and drink** between 12 and 2pm, every day except Monday when it is shut. There is a **phone box** at the western end of the village, in the wrong direction for Swale Way walkers. If all else fails, the lovely village green has a bench and plenty of space to lounge.

Maunby brings us about as close to the Swale as we've been since Fawdington, yesterday afternoon. We don't stray far from its course now, until journey's end.

Part 2 - Maunby to Morton-on-Swale

Approx 4½ miles (7 km) - 2 to 3 hours

1. Walk through the quiet, leafy village to reach the triangular green, with its tall trees. Bear right at the fork before the green, then immediate right again, into Pickeringmoor Lane.

2. Follow the lane, past the tiny Methodist Chapel, between tall hedges, and out into open countryside again. The fields appear to stretch for miles in every direction.

You may be able to see the stepped profile of Penhill to your left between the trees, almost 20 miles away. This overlooks the River Ure and Wensleydale in the Yorkshire Dales and can be visited as part of the Yoredale Way (see page 7).

3. It's impossible to get lost along Pickeringmoor Lane. It's almost exactly one mile from the last isolated house outside Maunby (SE 34866 86589), past the drive to Stubthorn House and the beautifully manicured lawns of Maunby Demesne, to the end of the lane at Rush Farm.

4. Here we may find a wide metal gate across our path and a small footpath marker (SE 34028 87834) pointing us left, through a double metal gate into a field.

5. Head half right across the field and climb the embankment which allows us to gratefully rejoin with the Swale. The right of way actually runs beside the field boundary fence, but the bank gives us better views and is easier to walk on. I doubt anyone will mind this minor trespass, other than the sheep.

6. Walk the embankment for exactly one mile, leaving it only briefly to pass through one gate on the way, until we reach a wire fence across our path (SE 33146 88604). Drop

down to a metal gate with a blue Swale Way marker that points us half right through the next field.

7. Aim for the far end of the line of small trees that make up the field boundary on the right. Here we find a wide metal gate (ignore the double red gates) leading to a grassy track between low hedges.

8. Follow the track for about 350 yards, passing through two more metal gates and into the yard of Far Fairholme farm. Continue straight ahead, through the yard and the track becomes a tarmac lane, Fairholme Lane.

To our left, across the river, is RAF Leeming, an airfield built in the Second World War for Bomber Command and still in operation today.

9. Another 350 yards, along the lane and we come to the buildings of Fairholme, a mixture of old and new to the right of the lane. A few dozen yards beyond these and we pass through a pair of brick gate posts (SE 32558 89866).

10. Stay on the tarmac lane, now called Potter Lane, for another mile and a half, until we reach the A684 (SE 32045 91815). Where we turn right along the road.

11. It's a little under ½ a mile into the village proper and we pass the start of tomorrow's path, on our left, as we proceed. If you haven't managed to secure one of the few beds in Morton, there are good transport links to Northallerton and Bedale from here.

MORTON-ON-SWALE

Morton-on-Swale is recorded in the Domesday Book as "Moretun". Its name being derived from the Old English words for moor "Mor" and farm "Tun", thus meaning Moor Farm on the River Swale.

As well as having its own **accommodation** in the form of **The Granary B&B** (Tel: 01609 773097 or 07703 545164) and the **Old Royal George Inn**, it has a frequent bus service to larger towns only a short distance away.

The number **73 bus** runs between Northallerton and Bedale, stopping at Morton every 30 minutes or so during the week and almost as frequently on Saturday. On a Sunday, the **856 service** runs between Hawes and Northallerton, but it's a limited service, so check the latest timetable carefully.

As well as providing beds, the Old Royal George also has a **bar** and a **restaurant** for non-residents. Check their website for opening times and special offers: **www.theoldroyalgeorge.co.uk**

About a mile further along the A684 is the village of **Ainderby Steeple** where additional **accommodation** may be available at the **Wellington Heifer**. A bed here, if nothing can be found in Morton, may save a bus journey.

SECTION THREE - MORTON-ON-SWALE TO RICHMOND
Approx 15 miles (24 km) - 6 to 8 hours

A little more up and down than the last two days, today's walk begins to ease us into the hills of tomorrow. Sticking close to the Swale as much as possible, we use field boundaries and riverside paths for most of the day, only resorting to tarmac for a couple of unavoidable sections. We visit the grave of a man reputed to have lived 169 years and reach the gateway to the Yorkshire Dales, Richmond; with its towering castle and the first waterfalls of the Swale.

PART 1 - MORTON-ON-SWALE TO GREAT LANGTON
Approx 4 miles (6 km) - 1½ to 2 hours

1. After joining the A684 at the end of yesterday's walk, we turned right along it. After 100 yards look out for a track between the houses on the left, marked by a vertical public footpath sign on a pole.

If you're walking from the village, there is another public footpath that appears to cut the corner and meet our path, on the other side of the railway. Indeed, the OS map shows two footpaths crossing the railway - neither of these should be relied upon. Instead use the track (SE 32208 92135), directly between the two, to cross the railway line (see below).

---

2. Follow the track between the houses and stay on it when it bends right behind them, ignoring the public footpath shown on the map, that should head straight through the field. The track passes an old brick building and runs beside a wooden post and rail fence on our left, to a metal gate that gives on to a railway crossing.

The railway looks disused, with weeds growing amongst the rails and sleepers, but this is the Wensleydale Railway, a tourist and heritage line running between Northallerton and Redmire. Very few trains run over the section of track we are crossing, with most services only coming as far east as Leeming Bar.

---

3. Cross the railway line and go through the gate on the other side, staying on the track between the fence on the left and the field on the right. About 300 yards after crossing the

railway, the track bends left through a pair of metal gates. Look for a stile (SE 32159 92408) with a yellow footpath marker, that allows us to continue ahead, into the field beyond.

4. Follow the field margin, with a fence and then bushes on our right, down to a concrete bridge over New Dike. Cross the bridge and bear left on the other side, keeping to the right-hand side of this field too.

5. Follow the edge of the field until we reach a large thorn bush with a stile beneath it. Our path continues directly ahead, over the stile and straight across the next field. Pass to the left of the power pole and look out for a hole in the hedge ahead of us (SE 31995 92838).

6. Follow a narrow path with a wooden fence on the left and a thick hedge on the right. After about 100 yards the path reaches a flight of stone steps and an alley leads us out to a residential street. We are entering Thrintoft village.

7. Turn right along the street for 100 yards or so until we reach a road junction. The road straight ahead leads us to the **New Inn pub** (closed Monday), but we need to turn left, along the road, away from the village.

8. Navigational duties can be suspended for the next couple of miles, as we follow the quiet Bramper Lane. There are no riverside paths along this section and we don't get a good view of the Swale until just before Catterick Bridge.

About a mile out of Thrintoft (SE 30945 94330), to the left of the road, behind the hedge, is an oxbow lake. This interesting geological feature was formed when a wide meander of the river was isolated by a change in the course of the water flow. Access is difficult and reveals little, but the shape of the lake is shown clearly on the OS map.

---

9. Just after Poole's Waste, the road bends sharply right and rises gently through fields. Look out for deer and hares in the fields and buzzards quartering the skies above. As we approach a bend in the lane (SE 31114 95095), look left and a gap in the hedges reveals Langton Hall.

> Originally called Langton Lodge, the building was constructed in 1770 by Leonard Smelt. In 1851 it was bought by Lord Teignmouth and extended in the gothic style, at which point it was renamed Langton Hall. In 1961 all of the gothic extensions were removed and the hall returned to its original state.

10. A few dozen yards further on we pass Langton Cottages, where you will find one of the most unusual garden ornaments in the country. Continue along the lane.

11. Another 200 yards or so and we reach a road junction. Turn left onto the lane, then keep right, ignoring the entrance to the Langton estate, instead following the quiet country lane. Despite the tarmac this can be a lovely walk. The woods beside the road have bluebells at the right time of year and the smell of wild garlic pervades the air.

12. About ¾ of a mile after the junction, we reach a war memorial beside the road (SE 30046 96061), opposite a track that leads to St. Wilfrid's church. Just beyond we get a rare glimpse of the Swale, through the trees beside the road.

13. A couple of minutes later the road takes us into the tiny village of Great Langton.

Part 2 - Great Langton to Bolton-on-Swale

Approx 4 miles (6 km) - 1½ to 2 hours

1. There is nothing in the village to slow our progress, except perhaps the benches on the tiny village green. Opposite the green is a lane and it's into this we turn right, off the road (SE 29484 96415).

2. The lane bends left in front of a house, then runs beside a tall hedge on the right, down to another house with a metal gate and a finger post. Follow the footpath through the garden of the house to a gate beneath a large tree at the bottom of the garden.

3. The gate gives on to an unkempt path through a small wood. Follow this for a few yards, to a rather confusing double stile. The path beyond this stile is almost impossible to follow; the footpath lies between the hedge

and the fence but is completely overgrown. Unless this has been rectified, use the second part of the stile to enter the field on the right and follow the fence you just crossed.

4. At the end of the field, use the wide metal gate (SE 29404 96835) and return to the public footpath. Bear slightly right through this large field, aiming for the left-hand edge of the clump of trees on the horizon to our right.

5. Here we find a stile set in the fence beneath the trees, which leads us into another field, now with a hedge on our right. Follow the field boundary, until it bends left in front of us, where we drop down, through a gap in the hedge to a gate.

6. Go through the gate and turn left into the next field. Almost immediately, turn right, in front of the hedge ahead of us. The path runs beside the hedge for about 500 yards until it meets a track cutting directly across our path (SE 29587 97734). Turn left onto the track.

The derelict building on our left is named Stanhowe Cottages on the OS map, but it's unlikely to be here for much longer, based on its current state.

---

7. After just a few dozen yards the track bends right through a wide gate. There is an information board here, listing some of the environmental projects Stanhow Farm has been working on. There's also a book for comments, should you wish.

8. We don't follow the track through the gate, instead we keep straight ahead, following the field boundary for another 500 yards or so, until we reach a gate. Go through this and continue ahead, now with the field boundary on our left.

9. Keep going straight, for about ½ a mile, until the hedge on the left becomes a wood, and we soon reach a track leading into the trees (SE 28352 97975). After a few yards this track emerges onto a gravel lane at Ladybank House.

10. Follow the gravel lane past the house and a little distance later, a cattle grid and a wide metal gate. Stay on the gravel lane until a pair of metal gates deliver us to the B6271 road.

11. Turn right onto the road, which we will follow for the next ¾ of a mile. Despite its "B" rating, this can be a busy road, but there is a good verge beside it for most of the way, which will help keep us out of the traffic.
12. We pass the entrance to Kiplin Hall about 600 yards along the road. There's a tea room here, as well as the chance to visit the house, grounds and gardens, should you wish.

Supposedly built from designs by Inigo Jones (the foremost architect of his time), Kiplin Hall stands in impressive grounds beside the River Swale. It was built around 1625 by George Calvert, later Lord Baltimore, who was Secretary of State for King James I. He was later to found the colony of Maryland in North America. Find more information: **www.kiplinhall.co.uk**

13. 600 yards or so beyond Kiplin Hall, just before the stone parapet of the bridge over Bolton Beck, keep an eye out for a finger post to the right of the road, pointing into the hedge. Here you will find a narrow, wooden gate that leads to a wide, metal gate.
14. Go through both gates, to enter a field and follow the hedge on the right, for about 450-500 yards, to another metal gate, with a stile beside it. Follow the lane beyond, past the houses, to a road junction.
15. Turn left onto the road for maybe 200 yards until we reach the red brick parapet of another bridge, also over Bolton Beck. Here we meet Wainwright's Coast to Coast (C2C) path for the first time and a finger post pointing us right, into a field.
16. Drop down from the road and through the wooden kissing gate. The yellow waymarker seems to suggest we should be on the left side of the fence that has recently been added to this field. However, this becomes very overgrown in the summer and difficult to negotiate. If this is the case, ignore the wide wooden gate and keep close to the fence on your left through this pasture.
17. After about 300 yards we reach a narrow wooden gate, cross a road and continue through another gate on the

other side of the road. In the next field, keep beside the fence on our left.

18. Another 300 yards brings us to a wooden kissing gate and an ancient brick bridge (SE 25822 98695) that takes us to the other side of Bolton Beck. Once across, follow the C2C marker which points us right along the field boundary, until we reach a kissing gate in the hedge in front of us. Go through this.

19. In the next field, continue with the beck on our right. The field boundary brings us to another wooden kissing gate, this one set in a wire fence. The path beyond hugs the beck, but as you will see, many people cut the corner and an obvious green path can be followed, half left across the field, towards a line of low trees.

20. At the trees we meet the beck again, which we can follow to another kissing gate set in the corner of the field (SE 25384 99174). Turn left onto the road beyond, heading for Bolton-on-Swale.

PART 3 - BOLTON-ON-SWALE TO RICHMOND

Approx 7 miles (11 km) - 3 to 4 hours

BOLTON-ON-SWALE

Bolton-on-Swale is mentioned in the Domesday Book as "Boletone". There is little in the way of amenities for a walker, but it's a famous point on Wainwright's Coast to Coast walk, mainly because of the memorial to Henry Jenkins (see below). There may still be a **self-service tea room** in the church and a bench beside the village pump, near the B6271.

1. The road takes us straight to the gate of St. Mary's church. It's worth cutting through the church yard for more than one reason. There's a self-service tea room in the church and if this isn't incentive enough then you may also want to visit the memorial to Henry Jenkins.

Henry Jenkins is a fascinating character, who supposedly died at the age of 169 years. As unlikely as this sounds, there is some evidence to support the claim. He is thought to have been born in 1500. He helped transport arrows destined for the Battle of Flodden in 1512. He gave evidence at a trial in York where his age was given as 140 and again in 1667 appeared as a witness in court. As well as the memorial in the church yard, there is a marble plaque on the wall inside the church.

sketched by Richard Collier

The memorial to Henry Jenkins

2. Refreshed (with tea) and astounded (by the life of Henry Jenkins) continue through the church yard and exit via the lych gate into the lane, straight ahead up to the main road.

3. Turn right onto the B6271, keeping to the pavement on the right. After about 50 yards, look for a wide vehicle

track on the left-hand side of the road. Cross over and follow this track.

4. The rough track bends right and then left and soon meets another, better track. Ahead of us is a huge sand and gravel quarry with a lake filling much of it. Turn right along the new track for about 350 yards. Just before we reach the main road, turn left, aided by a finger post (SE 24569 99594), along a green path beside a hedge on our right.

5. The path soon runs between trees, but then emerges at a metal gate, immediately followed by a wooden gate and continuing beyond. A few dozen yards beyond and we use another wooden gate to enter a large car park.

6. Turn right, out of the car park and then left, on a footpath beside the road, for about 40-50 yards to a finger post. This points us left, through the hedge, a metal gate, a short descent between fences and another metal gate, into a wide sunken pasture. The trees on our left hide the Swale.

7. A well-defined path runs beside the trees, offering much-welcomed views of the slow moving Swale on our left. About ½ a mile after entering the pasture, the path goes over a bank, (SE 23485 99730) between thorn bushes and into another field.

8. The path takes us through a wide metal gate. We are now constrained between wire fences for 200 yards or so, until the fence on the right ends. The path splits here and we keep left, soon walking between wire fences again.

9. We pass a large pond on the right, presumably the result of earlier quarrying activities. At the far end of the pond we meet a wooden fence and cross a low stile to enter a wide field. Keep to the left of the field, a hedge to our left, power cables running over our heads.

10. We cross another stile and after a couple more minutes arrive in sight of Catterick Bridge. A narrow, rusty gate gives on to the A6136 road (SE 22727 99424).

Catterick Bridge, or "Cataractonium" as it was called by the Romans, is a site of remarkable archaeological interest, far too extensive to be covered in this book. Originally a settlement of the Brigantes, it was of obvious strategic importance and soon taken over by the Romans, to control access into and out of Swaledale. It continued to be an important location, long after the Romans left.

It was at Catterick Bridge that Saint Paulinus, the first Bishop of York, took to baptising Christians in the River Swale. During his tenure, between 625AD and his hurried departure to the south in 633AD it is said he brought tens of thousands into the church in this way. As recently as 2014, the Bishop of Knaresborough, Rev. James Bell has held open air baptisms in the River Swale near Richmond.

11. Cross the road and go through a kissing gate beside a finger post. Keep straight ahead along a tarmac footpath to reach a rusty iron art installation commemorating soldiers through the ages. Climb the concrete steps and turn left onto a footbridge over the Swale.

12. At the far side, turn left down the steps and then left again to find a track that leads us to a kissing gate directly under the bridge we just crossed. Go through this and past the stone-brick River Gauging Station on the left.

13. Just beyond this we pass through another wooden kissing gate and keep ahead with trees on our right. The path now goes through a metal gate, uses a wide underpass beneath the busy A1 and arrives at another metal gate with a C2C marker on the wooden post beside it.

14. Using the direction of the marker, head half left, up the steep grassy bank towards a large farm shed on the skyline. Bear right, in front of the farm buildings and use a red metal gate to leave the yard (SE 22346 99168).

15. The path continues between a gap in the trees ahead, confirmed by the presence of a finger post. Looking down to your right reveals the Swale and beyond it, the buildings of Brompton-on-Swale.

16. We are now walking between a post and rail fence on the left and bushes on the right. Continue for about 150-200 yards, at which point we pass through a metal gate and the path widens a little. After another 150-200 yards the track

we are on bends downhill to the right. Ignore this, keep left alongside the fence.

17. Follow the fence for 300-350 yards, until our progress is halted by a fence across our path. We need to bear right here, following a narrow path beneath the encroaching trees for a few dozen yards to a narrow metal gate (SE 21579 99364).

18. Go through this, bear right and keep to the field boundary, following the fence on our right. After 350 yards the fence reaches a metal gate. Go through this.

19. In the tiny corner enclosure, keep to the fence on the right and after 50-60 yards we arrive at a metal gate with a finger post beside it. Use this to join a tarmac lane for a few short yards, before using another metal gate to enter a field on the right of the road.

20. A C2C finger post and a thin, but well-worn path indicates our direction across the field. You can see the red tiled buildings of St. Giles Farm away to the left and after 500 yards or so, we reach another metal gate. Go through this and keep to the left, beside the hedge, in the next field.

21. We stick to the hedge for another 500 yards until we reach a metal gate. Here we turn left, still following the line of the hedge. At the bottom of the field (SE 20316 99244), bear right and follow a wide vehicle track. The track runs for about 400 yards before reaching what looks like a turning area for farm vehicles. Here we find a blue footpath marker on a post, pointing us across the open area to another metal gate.

22. Go through this and follow the tarmac to the road. A finger post, on the other side of the road, points us right along it. After 100 yards, the road forks and we turn left, where we find the **Hildyard Arms** pub. Camping is available in the grounds if you use the pub, which is open from noon each day.

23. A few yards beyond the pub, the road splits into three. We take the middle option, the one with the blue road sign, showing a dead end. Follow this for a few dozen yards

until we reach the gates of a house and a C2C finger post, which points us down a path beside a wall.

24. All too soon this charming little path delivers us to a wooden kissing gate, which gives on to a wide field. Bear right across the field or use the field boundary to make your way up towards a pair of tall trees. Here you will find a metal kissing gate (SE 19228 99094) into the field beyond.

25. The path should be fairly obvious, even if the field is planted and within 150 yards or so we reach another C2C finger post and a wooden gate. The field beyond seems to be permanent pasture and the path is well worn, as it curves behind a power pole in the bottom left of the field.

26. A little way beyond the pole, at a wide, open gate the path becomes a vehicle track and heads gently uphill between trees.

27. After 100-150 yards the trees thin out and the track begins to bear away to the left. A thin path is visible heading slightly to the right, between two trees, but we need to turn more right (SE 18671 99305), past strewn rocks, along what quickly becomes an obvious path. A curtain of thorn bushes, low shrubs and trees, right beside the path, blocks our view of the Swale below.

28. The path descends gently to a wooden kissing gate where it enters a shady wood. In the spring and early summer, wild garlic and bluebells abound and the woods are a lovely place to be. Over the next 500-600 yards the path descends through the trees to meet a long flight of steps, crosses a wooden bridge and runs down to reunite us with the Swale. After a couple more tiny bridges we come to a wooden gate into a field.

29. The path through the field is fairly obvious and after a few yards it meets a green metal fence, running beside a sewage works. Follow the fence until it delivers us to a gravel road. Turn left along this for 20-30 yards until you see a finger post in the grass on the left of the road. Opposite this is another gravel track that leads us down to a cattle grid and a metal gate (NZ 18197 00172).

30. The track on the other side of these, is part of the old disused railway into Richmond, now a multi-use path for walkers and cyclists alike. Turn left along this and follow it for about ½ a mile to reach **The Station**.

The Station is the old Victorian railway building; brought back to life as an important community venue for groups, meetings and classes, and home to a variety of independent businesses. More importantly, from a walkers' perspective, there is food, drink and ice cream to be found here!

31. Leaving the Station, join the A6136, the main road into Richmond and cross the Mercury Bridge. There's a view of the Castle Keep and walls from here and the wide Swale running beneath. As we reach the far side of the bridge, look out for a gap in the parapet (NZ 17529 01016), that drops us down to the park beside the river.
32. Follow the riverside path to visit Richmond Falls, from where various routes can be found to take you uphill, into the town itself.

RICHMOND

Richmond is a wonderful town, in fact it was named UK town of the year in 2009. It was founded in 1071 on land granted to Alan Rufus by William the Conqueror. He promptly built a castle, to dominate the area, which was completed in 1086. It has remained an important place ever since.

The services available to a walker in Richmond are almost too long to list. There is **accommodation of all types**, for all budgets, but in the summer months the popularity of Wainwright's Coast to Coast walk means this can become scarce, so it's worth booking in advance.

There are enough hostelries for a serious pub crawl and at the weekend there are plenty of people doing just this. There are various take-away food options including **Pizza** and **Fish & Chips**.

Several shops offer **groceries**, snacks and other ingredients for a packed lunch. There are butchers, **bakers** and coffee makers,

high street bank branches with ATMs and a **Boots Pharmacy**. If you've lost or broken items of equipment or clothing, there's also an **outdoor shop**.

Just outside the town is **The Station**. This was the site of the old railway station and now includes a three-screen **cinema, café bar and restaurant**, artisan food stalls, including excellent **ice cream** and a chance to look back at the history of the town.

Richmond has plenty of **car parking**, both short term and long. A disc system is used, which provides two hours free parking in the town centre. Discs can be obtained from most shops and should be displayed in the car. Pay and Display is available a short walk from the centre, where anything from an hour to a week-long stay can be purchased.

With **good public transport** options, Richmond may be a place to stop for a couple of nights, using the bus to get to and from the Swale Way path in the morning and evening.

SECTION FOUR - RICHMOND TO REETH

Approx 12½ miles (20 km) - 5½ to 7½ hours

Today's walk begins beside the Swale with an undulating walk through some lovely woodland, followed by a steep climb, on steps up to the open moorland on the way into Downholme. Here we can stop for lunch in the Bolton Arms before we head out on one of the finest moorland paths anywhere in the Dales, around the edge of Stainton Moor. We pass another pub in Grinton before our arrival in the busy market town of Reeth.

Part 1 - Richmond to Downholme

Approx 5½ miles (9 km) - 2½ to 3½ hours

1. There are plenty of ways to leave the market square in Richmond, but if you follow the tarmac road rather than any cobbled wynds you will find the way. Head downhill with the Talbot Hotel on the right.

2. Keep to the tarmac of New Road and head even more steeply downhill. The road soon bends sharp left and becomes Bridge Street. A couple of hundred yards later we can see the bridge which the street is named after.

Built in the late 18th century it's known locally as the "Green Bridge". The bridge was designed by Yorkshire architect John Carr in 1788 and was so called because it crosses to what used to be Richmond's village green.

3. A fine view of Richmond Castle is available as we cross the wide, slow-moving Swale and turn right, beside a green gate (NZ 16959 00560) onto a footpath that takes us on a woodland walk, hard beside the river.

4. After a few yards we arrive at an information board and a choice of path. Avoid the cobbled stone path that keeps close to the river, as it's slippery and broken in places; keeping instead to the easier track on the left. This rises gradually above the river, through trees, beside impressive stone crags and old quarries. The walk through the wood is lovely, but the view of the river is somewhat restricted by the trees.

5. After a short distance the woodland path forks; keep to the right, heading gently downhill until we meet a wooden bridge at Billy Bank Wood. Cross the bridge and keep left, the steps to the right take us back to the riverside path we avoided earlier.

6. Another couple of hundred yards along the wooded path and we meet another fork; keep right here, heading downhill towards a gate. The gate takes us from the woods and into a green pasture. Walk straight ahead until we meet the Swale.

7. Turn left and walk beside the river on a wide path that runs for a couple of hundred yards to a kissing gate, beyond which we are channelled between the wooded hillside of Round Howe on our left and more trees, screening the river, on our right.

8. We soon arrive at a wide wooden gate, at Hudswell Woods (NZ 15739 00802). Here we find more information boards, a footbridge across the river and a choice of paths. Ignore the path that climbs away to the left, keeping right, level for a short distance and then dropping down to the river on a flight of tricky stone steps.

9. For the next ¾ of a mile we follow a wide path through the woods with the river on our right and the steep wooded slopes of Hudswell Bank on our left. Ignore any side paths up the bank, until, about 600-700 yards along its length there is a fork in the path, where we keep left, heading gently uphill away from the river.

10. We soon arrive at Hudswell Steps. Take a deep breath and begin the long climb. Counting the steps may or may not help take your mind off the ascent; there are a lot of them!

The steps were originally built by German prisoners of war during WWII and were completely renovated in 2016 by the Dales National Park and volunteers from various groups including cadets from Harrogate Army Foundation College.

11. Eventually the steps are interrupted by a track passing left to right in front of us (NZ 14513 00426). Turning left would bring us to Hudswell and the award-winning

George & Dragon, but it's probably too early for lunch for anyone walking from Richmond. Instead turn right.

12. The track passes through a gate (broken and rotting beside the path at the time of writing), beyond which we keep left, climbing a narrow muddy path into the trees. The path runs along the top of the field, with occasional views down into the valley on our right.

13. After a couple of hundred yards the path passes through a gap in a wooden fence and enters the woods of Church Gill. Follow the path, left into the gill for a short distance until it drops down to cross the narrow stream (NZ 14246 00489).

"Gill" or possibly "Ghyll" is a local word for a ravine or stream, derived from the Old Norse term "gil" with the same meaning.

---

14. On the other side, we now use a Permissive Path across Ministry of Defence land. Follow the path for 200-300 yards, through Spring Wood until we reach a gate. Go through this, turn hard right across a narrow beck and keeping to the fence on the right, climb out of the woods.

15. Keep following the fence on the right, with the Swale below, occasionally visible between the trees. Pass a large patch of gorse on the left and then bear left, uphill, still beside the fence on the right, towards a fence line that will soon become visible.

Turn for a moment here and look back at Richmond; a view you now share with the famous landscape artist, Turner, who painted the scene in 1816.

---

16. Cross the fence, using an awkwardly positioned stile and preview the rest of our route on the MOD information board showing the Thorpe Edge permissive path.

17. Keep the woods and fence on our right again. The field boundaries shown on the OS map for the next few hundred yards are now no more than a few thin lines of hawthorn bushes. The final boundary, beneath Scarcote Farm is a fence with a stile (NZ 13125 00735). Cross this and enter a wooded gill.

18. The exit from the gill isn't obvious, but keep straight ahead, using the fence on our right as a handrail and squeeze between the trees at the top of the bank, emerging into the field beyond. Leave the fence now, it heads right while we cut straight across the field, aiming for the line of trees to our front.

19. The permissive path is quite well marked. Go through the metal gate and follow the fence down into Scarcote Gill and back out again. Clear of the gill, look for the white arrow marker that now points us left, away from the fence, into the field, towards a stand of tall trees on the skyline.

20. Before we reach the trees another white-topped marker post guides us right, along a raised track. After only a few yards, a line of stones, possibly the remains of an old wall, guide us half left, uphill towards a gate in a wall, beneath the stand of tall trees. The first of a series of finger posts is situated beside the gate.

21. Beyond the gate turn left onto a vehicle track which heads gently uphill towards a line of telephone poles. Our second finger post points us beneath the telephone wires, out across the moorland of Thorpe Edge. The path across the moor is thin, but visible and the finger posts are close enough together (in good visibility at least) to aid progress.

Watch for bell pits, a relic of the old Swaledale lead mining industry. Do not go into the centre of these as sometimes the grass covers and disguises a mine shaft.

---

22. Our next finger post is soon visible on the skyline and beyond it the moor levels out a bit and the path becomes more obvious. Views down into Swaledale are somewhat restricted by the trees, but we will regain them soon.

23. Still heading west, after about 400 yards we reach the fourth finger post (NZ 12217 00403), which points us south west, towards a large plantation of conifers. Here we find a wide wooden gate set in a dry stone wall.

24. Go through the gate and follow the path that now skirts the plantation on our right, guided by posts with the white permissive path arrow on them. There is a fairly obvious

sheep trod beside the fence on the right, which protects an MOD conservation area. In May, these woods are carpeted with thousands of bluebells.

25. We can follow the path beside the fence for approximately 400-500 yards, until the fence begins to drop into a gully ahead of us.

26. Don't follow the fence into the gully, but head more left, across the tussocky grass towards two trees at the head of the gully (SE 11747 99608). Here, a good path with a marker post, takes us over the tiny stream and into the rough pasture beyond.

27. With the fence and the wooded gully to our right, we follow a clear path towards another white-topped post beside a broken wall. The path beyond sticks close to the edge of White Scar and the views down into Swaledale now become vast and impressive.

Here we can look down onto the wonderful view of Marske, a much bigger village in the old lead mining days (there were 3 smelt mills here), and the dales beyond.

---

28. After 500-600 yards we reach another white-topped post and 100 yards beyond that is a wide wooden gate and a stile (with a handy dog-slot) for walkers. Note the direction of the white arrow on the way marker.

29. Head half right away from the stile, ignoring the clear path that heads slightly left. Descend gently, across the long grass until we meet another path, running along a flat ledge overlooking the valley below. Turn left along this path.

30. Approximately 300-400 yards from the stile you should come upon a series of green humps and bumps on your left (SE 11340 98605) - this is White Earth, an area of lead mine prospecting. The path is much clearer now as it contours the slope of the hill.

31. Another 300-400 yards brings us to a double finger post. Look down to the right and see the enclosed churchyard of St Michael & All Angels, which dates from about 1180.

32. After the double finger post, look for a fork in the path where we bear right, down to a stile in a dry stone wall, with a yellow quarry warning sign on it. The quarry is now a local nature reserve and very picturesque.

33. Follow the clear path, past a small stone hut and then a smaller green metal box, with a toilet inside - which is odd! A little further on and we pass through a wide wooden gate, into a field. Keep beside the wall on the right until another wide wooden gate lets us out onto a tarmac track.

34. Turn right onto the track and follow it into the village of Downholme.

DOWNHOLME

Downholme is an ancient village, originally recorded in the Domesday Book as "Dune", which derives from the Old English word *Dun*, meaning hill.

Its main amenity for walkers is the Bolton Arms pub which is open from 11:30am to 3pm every day except Tuesday and from 6pm onwards, seven days a week. It's perfectly situated for a lunch stop for anyone who's walked from Richmond and both food and drink are available to replenish energy stores.

The pub is named after the local Lord Bolton of Bolton Castle, Wensleydale. More recently the whole village, pub and all, belonged to the Ministry of Defence as it is surrounded by a military training area.

If you can't walk any further you may be lucky enough to secure one of the two rooms in the pub, for the night. Alternatively, a phone box is available (at the time of writing) to ring for a taxi to Reeth.

A bus stop is situated at the far end of the village, outside the Vicarage. Services to Reeth, Richmond, Ripon and Leyburn are available here, using the 30, 159 or 610R services. Full details can be found at **www.traveline.info**

PART 2 - DOWNHOLME TO GRINTON
Approx 6 miles (9.7 km) - 2½ to 3½ hours

1. Follow the road past the Bolton Arms, down to the triangular village green where we meet the A6108, the main road between Richmond and Leyburn. Bear left onto the main road and after maybe 100 yards turn off right into a wide farm drive.

2. Follow the drive down to the farm yard, but bear right at the end into a good track between hedges. This is Stop Bridge Lane, which we follow for almost a mile. About half way down its length we cross a blue metal footbridge over the surprisingly wide Gill Beck.

3. At the end of the lane we reach a quiet tarmac road, onto which we turn right and head downhill for a short distance. If this was Open Access land we could use the red metal gate into the field on our left, to take the sting out of the climb we are about to make, but it's not, so we must continue downhill to the far gate in the same field.

4. A tall white flag pole is visible before we reach the metal kissing gate and the MOD warning signs that announce the access to the Public Right of Way (PRoW) that climbs up the hill (SE 09604 97340). The PRoW skirts the MOD Danger Area so even if the red flag is flying we can still use this path - just make sure you keep to the path and heed the warnings.

5. The path up the hill isn't obvious, but it hugs the fence on the right, beneath the trees, whose branches often impede easy progress up the steep climb. Take a breath at the top; we don't have much of a view, but any excuse will do!

At the time of most recent research, a pair of new metal gates were resting beside the wall at the top of the climb, presumably to be installed here. As such, the next point may change.

---

6. Turn sharp right at the top of the climb, go through a wooden gate and along the wall. Within a few yards we pass through another wooden gate and beyond this we aim for the left-hand corner of the wall ahead of us.

7. For the next 600-800 yards we keep the boundary wall of Scar Spring Wood on our right and the open green pasture on our left. MOD warning signs remind us that this is a

Military Firing Range, so don't touch any strange debris you may find!

8. We soon reach a stile in the dry stone wall which transitions us from pasture to open moorland. The path beyond is thin but clear, through an overgrown limestone quarry for a few yards, before bending left just before the last tree. What lies beyond is our first proper view of the splendour of Swaledale.

9. A lone standing stone (SE 08929 96918) identifies the boundary between the parishes of Ellerton Abbey and Stainton, but also marks a great stop for a sit down to admire the view.

Ellerton and Marrick Priories can be seen in the valley below. All that remains of the Cistercian Ellerton Priory is a church tower while the Benedictine Marrick Priory is now occupied by a Christian Outdoor Activity Centre.

---

10. Beyond the boundary stone, follow the thin path along the top edge of Ellerton Scar. A series of moss-covered wooden posts keep us on the best line as we progress from close-cropped grass to ankle deep heather. The path is well used, for obvious reasons - it's a truly wonderful place to be. Don't be fooled into following the fence line down to the face of the scar, keep towards the top of the slope - aim for the tops of the trees you should see poking out above the heather.

The moor is home to Curlew and Grouse. The haunting cry of the former is a stark contrast to the rattling cackle of the latter, but both add a wonderful soundtrack to the day's walk. Skylarks can also be heard, singing their hearts out as they hover high above us.

---

11. Perhaps 400-500 yards after the boundary stone these trees come fully into view, inside a walled enclosure, which we keep on our left and a couple of hundred yards beyond them the path starts to drop gently, through the heather past another finger post.

12. A further 300-400 yards and we reach another finger post (SE 08216 96436), now pointing us more right, downhill,

closer to the wall on our right. The PRoW is right beside the wall, but we're actually heading for the left-hand edge of the plantation of trees we can see ahead - the wall zig-zags down to it, but we can cut across using a number of handy sheep trods.

13. Once there we find a stile that leads to a thin path through the bracken, down into the steep gully of Juniper Gill. The storm of July 2019 badly eroded the beck here and the crossing of it may not be immediately apparent. Bear left up the gill for just a few yards then cross the beck and climb the steep bank up towards the tall juniper trees.

14. Here we find a wall and a path that may be hidden by bracken in the height of the summer, which we follow uphill beside the wall to another stile.

15. Over the stile, bear left, using a green path through the bracken, heading for a wide metal gate in the dry stone wall ahead. It soon becomes clear we aren't going through the gate, so keep left along the wall to reach another finger post.

16. Follow the wall around to the right and keep to the thin green path beside it. More MOD warning signs keep us hard against this wall for maybe 400-500 yards until we reach the next finger post, beside the ruins of a field barn (SE 07081 96326).

17. Views of Ellerton Moor to our left and Swaledale to our right combine to make this a lovely section of the path. 200-300 yards after the barn we pass another finger post and shortly after this look out for a cluster of poles in a fence line ahead. Head away from the wall, towards these, up to find a stile beside a finger post pointing left.

Note: In July 2019 devastating floods hit Swaledale. The Swale and its tributaries were filled with raging torrents as water falling on the surrounding hills was forced down their narrow confines. Bridges were destroyed, farmland flooded, livestock swept away and killed. The Swale Way crosses some of the tributaries affected by the storm waters and these have now become too dangerous to walk in due to the amount of loose rocks and large boulders and the risk of landslides.

The notes that follow are a significant change in route from the traditional Swale Way and will probably need to be in force for the foreseeable future, until nature can stabilise the conditions in the affected gills.

The crossing of **Hags Gill**, the use of **James Raw's Rake** and the crossing of **Cogden Beck** should all be avoided!

18. Cross the stile and turn left along an obvious track beside the fence line that climbs gently beside the deep defile of Hags Gill on our right. The gill is filled with loose rocks and large boulders that were deposited by the floods of July 2019.

19. After about 500 yards we reach a tarmac lane (SE 06394 95840) and turn right along it. The lane is little used and offers splendid views down into Swaledale and across Grinton Moor on our left.

This road was used as part of the *Grand Depart* for the Tour de France in 2014. The hill being dubbed Côte de Grinton Moor.

20. After a mile or so we reach the repaired bridge over Cogden Beck (SE 04833 96870). Looking at the size of the beck running below it is hard to imagine the volume of water that must have been needed to wash away the old stone bridge.

21. We follow the road for another ½ a mile until we reach Grinton Lodge Youth Hostel. Continue past the hostel and stay on the road until the wall on our right expires.

22. Here (SE 04724 97706) a finger post points us half right, off the road and down towards a wide gate between a pair of tall barns and a long, low barn to their right. Go through the gate into the field.

23. Continue downhill through the field and through the wide gate in the wall ahead of us. Beyond this we bear partly right, under the overhead cables to a narrow gate. Once through this you should see a field barn with a little gate to its right (SE 04808 98014). Go through this gate and follow the wall on the left down to a much wider gate.

24. A further 150 yards down through the next field will bring us to a narrow gate which gives on to the tarmac road, which we can cross and use the pavement into Grinton.

GRINTON

There are only a handful of buildings in Grinton and this has always been the case, so it seems unusual that such a small village should have such an imposing church as St. Andrews. Often called "The Cathedral of the Dales", it was originally built in the time of the Normans but has been added to over the intervening centuries. It is one of the most important medieval buildings in the whole of Swaledale and is Grade I listed. One of the grave stones in the churchyard is Grade II listed - that of Richard Clarkson - have a look, see if you can find it.

If you're interested in the industrial archaeology of the lead mining industry, **Grinton Smelt Mill**, a little way out of the village, dating from 1820 is a perfect place to explore.

A view of the restored buildings at Grinton Smelt Mill

The other building of importance in the village is of course the pub - the **Bridge Inn**. This offers accommodation if you don't think you can manage the remaining mile into Reeth. As its name suggests, the pub is situated right beside the bridge over the Swale.

The Bridge Inn serves food; both bar food and in a separate, fine dining restaurant section and an excellent selection of ales.

On the way into the village we passed the **telephone box** located on the B6270, beside the old Grinton Literary Institute building. Grinton's small **public convenience** building is situated just beside the telephone box.

There are two **bus stops**, located opposite each other, on the road behind the pub, next to the telephone box. Grinton is serviced by the following bus routes; 30, 36 and 480R running between Richmond and Keld.

About ½ a mile up the road (and the hill) is **Grinton Lodge Youth Hostel**, an old hunting lodge with plenty of space and large airy common rooms. If you stay here and wander down to the pub for a drink, remember to take a torch with you for the return journey - there are no street lights on the road up the hill!

Part 3 - Grinton to Reeth

Approx 1 mile (1.6 km) - 20 to 30 minutes

1. The road we follow into the village brings us to the Bridge Inn and St. Andrew's church. Follow the road around to the right and after 100 yards or so we cross the Swale on the fine old stone bridge.

The earliest part of Grinton Bridge is 16th century and was later widened in line with a design by John Carr, who you may remember from the 'Green Bridge' at the start of today's walk.

---

2. At the far side of the bridge, on the left-hand side, keep an eye out for a narrow gate that opens on to a steep set of stone steps (SE 04636 98569), leading down to a path between two fences.

3. Follow the path, it's difficult to do anything else, through a series of double gates, for around ½ a mile until we reach the road into Reeth.

Just before reaching the road into Reeth you pass on your right the 18th century Fremington corn mill, still with its water wheel.

4. A pavement beside the road keeps us safe from the traffic, until we reach another bridge over the Swale. This one is narrow, with no room for a pavement and the traffic can be busy, so pick your moment and cross when you can.

5. The pavement resumes on the other side of the bridge and we can follow this all the way into the village. Just before we arrive in the village proper you will find the Reeth Village Store, the first of many amenities in the village.

6. Continue up the hill until we reach the large village green, market place and the end of the day's walk.

REETH

Reeth is another town that can be dated as far back as the Domesday book. In there it was called "Rie" which is the ancient Anglo-Saxon name for a ditch, beck or river.

The most prominent feature of Reeth is its village green, a large, gently sloping expanse of well-maintained grass surrounded by picturesque shops, pubs and houses. Reeth is a great place to stock up on supplies, send a few postcards and sample some fabulous Black Sheep ale.

Reeth has ample accommodation options including **several B&Bs** and three **pub-type hotels** as well as a **hotel / restaurant** at the top of the village green. More detailed accommodation information can be obtained from the National Park Centre located in the village.

The village has three pubs, all located around the green; The **Black Bull**, the **Kings Arms** and the **Buck Hotel**; all are popular with walkers and offer food as well as traditional pub fare.

There is ample **parking** in Reeth around the central village green. A **telephone box** is located at the top of the village green (top meaning both north and most elevated end) beside the **bus stop** and **public toilets**. There are several **tea rooms** and even an **ice-cream parlour**. As with most of the facilities in the village the majority are located around the village green.

The **bus stop** at the top end of the village beside the Buck Hotel, is serviced by the following bus routes; 30, 36 and 480R running between Richmond and Keld.

There are three **general stores** in Reeth, one of which also includes the **Post Office**, situated on the east side of the green.

Water pump in Reeth, outside the Wesleyan Chapel

As well as the tea rooms and the pubs which all serve food there is also a **restaurant** at the very top of the village in the **Burgoyne Hotel**. The **Copper Kettle** tea room has an extensive menu including main meals.

Although there is no pharmacy in the village, the **Post Office** has basic first aid supplies and common "over the counter" medicines.

SECTION FIVE - REETH TO KELD
Approx 12 miles (19 km) - 5½ to 7½ hours

We're almost close enough to jump into the Swale for the first five miles of today's walk as we leave Reeth via the "Swing Bridge" and follow riverside paths to Low Houses and Isles Bridge. We climb the side of the valley to visit Smarber Chapel before dropping again into Gunnerside in time for lunch. Afternoon sees us hugging the river again using wide pastures and flood plains to reach the dramatic passage through Kisdon Gorge and the gentle climb up to the tiny village of Keld.

Part 1 - Reeth to Gunnerside
Approx 6½ miles (10.5 km) - 3 to 4 hours

1. There are plenty of ways to leave Reeth, but our route has the cobbled market square on the left and a row of shops with the Black Bull on our right and we head downhill.

2. A few short yards will bring us to Hudson House, the large white, multi-purpose building at the head of Anvil Square. Keep the tiny triangle of grass to our left as we walk through the square and bend right. A "To the River" sign on one of the houses ahead, points us down an alley.

3. The 'ginnel' brings us to a tarmac lane and at the end of that we turn left into a residential street. A couple of dozen yards along this and we arrive at a T-junction. Bear right, following the finger post for "Swing Bridge".

4. The tarmac we were walking on, peters out after a hundred yards or so, leaving us following a stony track with a raised pavement on the right. The impressive hill on our left is High Harker Hill, with the expanse of Harkerside Moor beyond.

The family name Harker is a common one in Upper Swaledale. As early as 1674 there were seven Harkers living in the Reeth area and a further twelve families of this name in the parish of Muker and Melbecks.

---

5. After another hundred yards or so and our path meets a pair of old green gates, with a narrow, muddy track

between walls bending down to our left (SE 03462 99127). Use this track, which can be slippery after rain.

6. Ahead, between the trees you should be able to see the Swale and once we reach the bottom of the walled track and pass through the gate beside the barn, we meet it again properly.

7. Bear right beyond the gate, crossing a duckboard bridge and then following a wide path between a 'forest' of newly planted trees on the left and a fence on the right. Follow this for around 200-300 yards until the impressive "Swing Bridge" comes into sight.

8. Pass through a wooden gate in a wall across our path and we arrive at the bridge. Despite its name, the bridge is not designed to swing, but it's still a wonderful structure.

The bridge we see today was built in 2002 after the previous span, which had survived for 80 years and innumerable floods, was destroyed by an uprooted tree being washed down the swollen river in September 2000.

---

9. Bounce your way across the river and turn right on the other side, following an unmarked path between the river and the fence. The Swale is wide and slow here and it's hard to imagine the level can rise 3 metres when it floods!

10. After 300-400 yards our progress is halted by a wooden fence across our path. Use the stile to cross it and continue beside the river on a smooth green path. We pass two trees, one of which has fallen and just beyond these we reach a public bridleway, marked with a wooden post (SE 02694 98891).

11. From this point our path is on a raised embankment with a thin screen of trees separating us from the river on the right. We pass through a gate and the embankment becomes more defined with the addition of a broken wall on our left.

12. About 200-300 yards beyond the gate, our path drops down to meet the river and becomes cobbled for a short distance, before returning to grass again. The houses of Healaugh should be visible through the trees. A couple of

hundred yards beyond the cobbles and you may see a set of stepping stones (SE 02082 98741) that connect this footpath to the one on the other side, leading up to the village. Only when the river is low are these actually usable.

13. Another hundred yards brings us to a gate in a wooden fence. Go through this and bear left, up a gentle slope to a wall, which we walk beside. The path climbs away from the river, providing excellent views of Healaugh, Calver Hill behind it and Swaledale.

14. Follow the green path beside the wall for about ½ a mile until we reach a metal gate with a stile beside it. Continue beside the wall for another 50-60 yards until it turns away sharp left and we bend less sharply left up to a gate beside a telephone pole (SE 01500 98352).

15. Beyond the gate our path rises between bracken and juniper bushes, emerging at a tarmac lane with a finger post pointing back to "Grinton 2¼ ml". Turn right along this very quiet road.

A short diversion is possible here, left along the road for 600-700 yards, then following the footpath from (SE 02020 98283) up the hillside to the Iron Age fort of Maiden Castle. Little remains to be seen however, other than the ditches and the tumbled stones of its impressive 110m entrance corridor.

16. The road offers some fine views up the valley and after about ½ a mile we cross Browna Gill and then a cattle grid. Another ¼ of a mile and we ignore the road to our right that passes over Scabba Wath bridge and continue ahead.

Scabba Wath is thought to be the name given to a foot ford used by Roman soldiers travelling from their fort in Bainbridge to their more permanent camp at Greta Bridge.

17. We pass some cattle sheds on the right of the road and ¼ of a mile after passing the right turn we arrive at a fork in the road at Low Whita (SE 00342 98202). There is a bunkhouse here. Take the right fork, along Low Lane.

18. Low Lane runs for 1½ miles between dry stone walls with intermittent views to the northern slopes of Swaledale and

the houses and field barns dotted all over it. The lane eventually brings us to Low Houses, a cluster of farm buildings, one of which bears the name of J. (James) Harker and a date of 1840.

19. A few yards beyond we come upon Lawn House, built in 1766 when the lead mining industry was producing incredible profits for the mine owners (SD 98213 97305).

More recently, Lawn House was the home of Thomas Armstrong (1899-78) author of "The Crowthers of Bankdam" and the locally set "Adam Brunskill".

20. Stay on the road for another 600-700 yards. Look across the dale and try to identify the cluster of buildings on the skyline, a dark line of wall running up to them. This is our next goal, the houses at Smarber.

The houses at Low Row

21. We pass a well-hidden telephone box and then turn right onto a tarmac lane, signposted "Reeth 4, Richmond 15". Follow the lane down to, and across, Isles Bridge.

Isles Bridge was first built in 1734, out of wood, but was washed away twice during floods. In 1801 a local farmer,

Section Five - Reeth to Keld 97

Richard Garth, raised money to build a stone bridge. This too was badly damaged by flood in 1883 and had to be rebuilt. The bridges of the Swale have to be of hardy construction!

22. Beyond the bridge the tarmac lane rises to meet the B6270 where we find a bench, but don't pause here. Instead, turn left along the road, looking for a set of wooden steps that appear in the wooded embankment on the right side of the road (SD 97723 97642). Climb the steps.

23. At the top of the steps, turn right through a wide wooden gate. A clear path rises away between the trees, follow this for 100 yards or so until it emerges into a field. Turn sharp left, almost back in the direction we came from, this time with the trees on our left, towards a gate in a dry stone wall ahead.

24. Beyond the gate our path contours the hillside. A look behind us reveals a sweeping view of Swaledale and the view ahead is no less impressive. After 500-600 yards we come to another gate, go through this and join the wall, keeping it to our right.

25. A few yards on and we come to a fine old stone barn. Just the other side of this is a walled enclosure. This is all that remains of Smarber Chapel. A stone plaque on the wall is all that identifies it.

The Toleration Act of 1689 allowed freedom of worship and many Dales folk chose to follow the Congregationalists and Presbyterians. Smarber Chapel, above Low Row was the first non-conformist chapel in Swaledale, built in 1690 by Phillip Lord Wharton, who owned local land and lead mines. It was replaced in 1809 by the Congregational Chapel in Low Row.

26. Retrace a few steps back from the chapel and you should see a wide wooden gate leading into a field (SD 97303 97571). Go through this and climb directly up towards a wide gate in the dry stone wall on the horizon, situated beside a row of small trees and a pair of poles carrying the power lines to Smarber.

27. Go through this gate and head half left in the next field, past the power pole, aiming for the field corner and another gate.

28. In the next field keep the wall to our right and after 150 yards or so aim for a narrow, gated stile in the wall across our path. In the next 100 yards, pass through two more open field boundaries. The view ahead now opens up with Upper Swaledale laid out before us and the bulk of Great Shunner Fell at its head.

29. The next narrow, gated stile takes us into Rowleth Wood (SD 96847 97748). The wood is lovely, especially in the height of summer, but the path through it can be slippery and awkward after rain. It's rare to be able to walk through woods in Upper Swaledale and this one is well cared for by the Low Row Pasture Committee. After a pleasant ½ mile we use a pinch stile to exit into a green pasture.

30. Cross what will probably be a dry beck and through a gap in another wall. Cross two more green fields using gaps in the walls, following the overhead cables and then over a stone step stile in a tall wall that brings us into a walled lane. From the top step of the stile (SD 95964 98188) you can see Gunnerside in the valley below.

31. A wide green lane takes us downhill now, past the remains of Lane Foot, which the information board tells us were two cottages, once owned by another Harker, Simon this time, who's family lived there for over 40 years.

32. Our wide green lane now becomes a stony, sometimes muddy, track which crosses a beck, bends left and then right and continues steeply downhill. After a hundred yards or so we pick up a wall on our left and another hundred yards brings us to a tarmac lane. Turn left, steeply downhill, through a narrow wooden gate into the village of Gunnerside.

33. Another hundred yards along the road and we find a pub and a tea room. Hopefully you've timed your arrival to coincide with lunch in the Kings Head.

Section Five - Reeth to Keld

GUNNERSIDE

Gunnerside is an Old Norse settlement and was also a centre for the lead mining industry. In fact, the village provides the easiest access to some of the best-preserved remains of the Swaledale mining industry.

The village itself is centred around its pub, the **Kings Head**. The pub sign suggests the king in question was a Viking and if the village's name is any clue, then his name would have been Gunnar.

There is also a tea room, next to the pub; the **Ghyllfoot**, which also includes the **Penny Farthing** restaurant. The village has a small number of **parking** places and a set of **public toilets**, just down the path beside the pub.

A small working **Smithy** is located in the village alongside an excellent **museum** showing local history.

Gunnerside is serviced by **bus route 30**; between Keld and Richmond. This service runs twice a day, Monday to Saturday to Keld, but more often to Richmond. At weekends and Bank Holidays, this is replaced by the **less frequent 830** service. Services and schedules are seasonal, so check availability before relying on a service.

In Old Norse, Gunnerside was "Gunnar's Saetr", so we must presume that it was a Norseman called Gunnar who first established the settlement. It is therefore quite apt that the King portrayed in the Kings Head pub sign is depicted as a Viking (he wouldn't have had horns on his helmet though!).

PART 2 - GUNNERSIDE TO KELD

Approx 5½ miles (9 km) - 2½ to 3½ hours

1. To leave the village, cross the bridge outside the pub and bear left for just a few yards. On the right-hand side of the road, look for a cluster of benches and an ancient stone trough on a small triangle of village green (SD 95082 98179). If you brought a packed lunch, this is a perfect place to sit in the sun and enjoy it.

2. Take the narrow lane behind the green, between the houses and follow it down towards the village school. Just before arriving at the school (on our left) you will see a wooden gate on the right with a "Footpath Ivelet" sign on it. Follow this between the houses to a narrow-gated pinch stile that gives out on to the fields beyond.

3. The path for the next 500-600 yards is clear as it crosses four field boundaries, using either stiles or gaps in the dry stone walls.

4. After the fourth boundary, a narrow, gated stile in a wall, the path approaches a wooden stile set in a wire fence. Ignore this, and the path beyond which drops down to the river, instead bear right, uphill beside the fence. We soon reach a gated gap in the wall at the top of the rise.

5. For the next ½ a mile the path is easy to follow as it crosses seven field boundaries using the now familiar spring-loaded, often vicious, always awkward narrow, gated stiles. We're aiming for a line of trees ahead, and a final gated gap in the wall beside a large field barn.

6. Go through the gate and drop down to a narrow footbridge (SD 93707 98012) over the lovely Shore Gill. Cross the bridge and climb up again to the tarmac road in Ivelet. Turn left along the road, after 50-60 yards turn left at a T-junction with a telephone box, then continue as it drops down and bends right for about 600-700 yards before arriving at Ivelet Bridge.

In this area, packhorses were the main form of goods transport until the 1880s. Fords were the usual ways of crossing rivers, but Ivelet is fortunate to have one of the finest packhorse bridges in the Dales. Dating from 1695, it is also reputed to be haunted by a headless dog.

Ivelet Bridge (also known as Satron Bridge) was part of the Swaledale Corpse Road (see page 40) and a coffin stone sits here, at the end of the riverside parapet. Mourners would rest here, standing the coffin on the stone, while they caught their breath.

7. We don't cross the bridge, we use the narrow gate in the stone wall ahead of us and follow the finger post "FP Muker" into the field. The path stays close to the river, screened by tall trees, until we reach a wide gap in the wall ahead and another finger post.

8. Rather than sticking to the left-hand edge of the field, which seems obvious, we bear gently right through this field aiming for the left end of the short section of wall running down from the tree line on the right. When we reach this, look for a gate in the field boundary ahead of us (SD 92875 97763).

9. In the next field, bear left, back towards the river and pick up a green path that sticks close to the Swale on our left for about 600-700 yards, passing through a gate and beside a field barn in the process.

10. The path narrows as the woods on the right encroach on the river and we go through a narrow gate and follow a thin path, made awkward by exposed tree roots, penned in between the now rushing Swale and the wooded slope.

11. After a hundred yards or so the little track deposits us back into meadow land and the fertile flood plain beside the river. Follow the obvious green of our new path through the field, initially beside a broken wall and then not, until after 600-700 yards we reach a narrow, gated stile in the wall ahead of us.

12. Go through the gate and continue ahead, aiming for a finger post sitting atop the embankment (SD 91757 97925), beneath a tall tree beside the river bank. The Swale is shallow here, running fast over stones to create white water and a perfect place for fording animals in the past.

13. Beyond the finger post we join a vehicle track for a short distance which takes us into the next field. Look for a stile in the wire fence on the left and use this to join a path between the river and the fence. After a short distance this brings us to a gated gap in a dry stone wall with a sign asking us to keep in single file through the fields beyond.

14. Another sign warns against fording the river here, suggesting the use of the bridge we are now heading for.

Head half right through the field, aiming for a gated gap in the wall to the left of a wide vehicle gate. Look for two more similar gates in the next two fields, each about 50-60 yards apart.

The green lump to our front, criss-crossed with dry stone walls, is Kisdon Hill. Every year, as part of the Muker Show, runners compete in a fell race, up and over Kisdon Hill and back to Muker. The winning time is usually less than 12 minutes!

---

15. A hundred yards beyond the third gate we reach the cluster of buildings at Ramps Holme Farm. To the left of the farmhouse, go through a small gap in the wall protected by a spring-trap gate (SD 91188 98296), up the grassy embankment and aim for the field barn surrounded by tall trees.

16. Another gated gap beside an ancient green metal gate leads to a muddy path beside a wire fence on our left. Follow this for 50-60 yards, bearing left where the path branches and then drops down to the Ramps Holme footbridge.

17. Cross the bridge and keep right on the far side. Another narrow gate and then a path between a wall and a fence leads us into the head of Swaledale.

A diversion into Muker (pronounced Mew-ker) is possible now; a flight of stone steps on our left (SD 90966 98633) lead up to a gate and a clearly laid path through the wonderful hay meadows, all the way into the village.

MUKER

Muker gets its name from Old Norse - in this case "Mjor-aker" or narrow acre. The Vikings farmed the area and this remained the major activity until the 1800s when lead mining became prevalent. Like Keld, just up the valley, Muker was a hub of mining activity. Upon its decline, farming took over again and now tourism plays a large part in the village economy.

One of the most traditional of all Yorkshire "shows" takes part in Muker in early September every year. Complete with Sheep

Dog trials, dry stone walling demonstrations and livestock competitions.

For such a small village Muker has a surprising range of local services. There is the excellent **Farmers Arms** pub which does bar meals at lunch and in the evening. Next door is a **tea room / restaurant / local shop** affair **Muker Village Stores**, which also does **B&B**. Across the road is a set of well-maintained **public toilets** and **telephone box**. A large **car park** is situated 50-60 yards beyond the village by the bridge.

Muker sits on the Service 30 **bus route** between Keld and Richmond, one stop along from Thwaite - this service runs only twice a day and varies seasonally.

18. If you're not going to Muker, ignore the steps and continue beside the wall to another gated gap. Beyond, keep the wall on our left and follow the path as it passes beside a field barn and into the wide valley.

The path that takes us up Swaledale must be one of the most beautiful anywhere in the Dales. The river is wide and slow and the surrounding hills are steep and become ever more narrow as we proceed. The path on our side of the river is much quieter than the one on the opposite side, that one being used by Wainwright's Coast to Coast as an alternative low-level route to Reeth.

---

19. A finger post just beyond the barn (SD 90813 98771) tells us to stay on the high side of the path. Over the next ½ a mile or so we pass through a narrow, gated gap, a couple of wide ungated gaps in walls, a wide metal gate, a muddy section with small stepping stones and finally a wide wooden gate with a "Please keep dogs on a lead" sign. Bear left beyond this gate.
20. For the next ½ a mile the path is easy to follow as it crosses several field boundaries, most of which are broken walls with the occasional intact one. We move away from the river, skirt a large conifer plantation on our left and a couple of derelict field barns before arriving at a point where the path appears to split (NY 90789 00177).

21. Keep left, with the mostly intact dry stone wall on our right and begin to climb the flank of what is quickly becoming a narrow valley.

The steep defile on the opposite side of the valley is Swinner Gill; a beautiful path that takes walkers up onto the open moorland of Melbecks Moor - this is visited as part of the **Herriot Way**, covered in another book by this author.

Also visible on the other slope is the now mostly derelict Crackpot Hall. Originally built as a Hunting Lodge in the 16th century and modified in the 18th century as a farmhouse, the building was only abandoned in the 1950's due to subsidence.

22. Although the path, now climbing steadily, is not particularly well defined, it's fairly easy to follow as there isn't much in the way of alternatives. We pass a barn with a yellow blob of paint marking a footpath, a broken wall and then another field barn, this one with a finger post (NY 90485 00527). The path beyond is clear as it continues to climb.
23. Keep to the left of the broken wall as we climb the hillside, to join a slightly sunken track that passes between trees and then past a derelict building on our left, before reaching a gate in a very tall dry stone wall.
24. For the next 400-500 yards the stony path follows a very obvious vehicle track, ducking beneath low trees and continuing to climb gently. We soon meet a three-way finger post (NY 89804 00857) that introduces us to the Pennine Way for the first time and which we will follow into Keld.
25. The path drops a little now and a few yards beyond the Pennine Way finger post we find another, this time for Kisdon Force - a splendid series of waterfalls.

The optional diversion to Kisdon Force is an out-and-back affair, as there is no easy route into Keld other than by walking back up to the track we're on now.

26. Continue along the track until we pass through a gate and the path meets a wall from the left, which we follow for 300-400 yards into the tiny village of Keld.

27. One of the first buildings we find as we enter the village is **Park Lodge** farm. In the summer months they operate a tea room and tiny shop, selling snacks and drinks. In the winter months, to fill the gap, the village has opened the doors of the **Public Hall** (it has a yellow defibrillator box on its wall) and here you will find a self-service tea room.
28. If you prefer something stronger, head uphill (past Butt House B&B) to find Keld Lodge which will serve alcoholic drinks and provide a bed for the night.

There is some evidence of buildings in Keld dating back as far as the 17th century, with a barn in the field just to the east of the village sporting a 1687 datestone above its doorway. **Park Lodge** has an original datestone from 1760 and out-buildings that were added in each successive century.

The **two chapels** in the village and many of the other buildings sprang from the prosperity of the lead mining industry in the mid-19th century. Once this died away however, the village seems to have been forgotten as there is very little 20th century influence; probably not a bad thing at all.

KELD

Keld is more a cluster of buildings, a hamlet maybe, rather than a village. However, in terms of amenities it punches well above its weight; offering a **tea room**, a **pub**, a **telephone box** and **public toilets** where other, larger settlements have none of these.

There are relatively few beds in Keld, in comparison to the number of walkers that use the village. **Butt House** is the large farmhouse by the telephone box at the top of the village, close to the old Youth Hostel, now a hotel called **Keld Lodge**, which offers food and drink as well as rooms.

Keld Lodge also serves food to non-residents with an interesting menu and fantastic views from the large picture windows. **Butt House** provides an evening meal for residents.

Ample **parking** is available at the bottom end of the village, furthest from the main road, in the yard of **Park Lodge Farm**.

They charge a small fee and ask that you use the honesty box by the entrance of the car park to deposit your coins.

A **telephone box** is located on the edge of the village, between Keld Lodge and Butt House. There is no mobile reception in the village on any network.

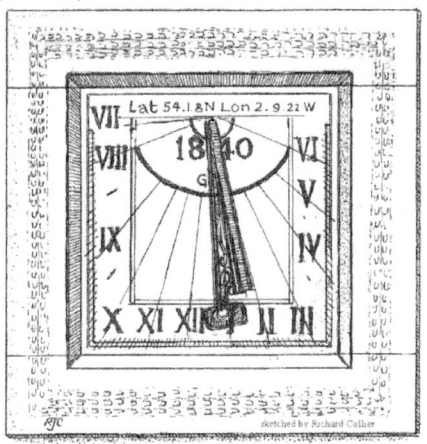

The Keld sundial, on the United Reformed Church

Keld Public Hall, at the bottom of the village, close to where our path arrives, has a community run **tea room** in the winter, that provides hot and cold drinks, a selection of locally made cakes and other supplies most welcome at the end of a long walk. There's plenty of seating in the hall, if it's raining.

The **bus stop** is located on the B6270 beside the **telephone box**, just down from **Keld Lodge**. Keld is serviced by the following bus routes; 30, 36 and 480R running to Richmond.

SECTION SIX - KELD TO KIRKBY STEPHEN
Approx 12½ miles (20 km) - 6 to 8 hours

Leaving Keld, we use farm tracks, field paths, old bridges and a short road section to help us achieve our goal of reaching the source of the Swale, in a remote junction of valleys. Another short road section, along the quiet and picturesque B6270 brings us to a moorland path and the long, steady ascent of Nine Standards Rigg, up to the iconic cairns that sit atop it. Here we can soak in the views before beginning the descent into Kirkby Stephen and journey's end.

PART 1 - KELD TO THE SOURCE OF THE SWALE

Approx 3½ miles (5.5 km) - 2 to 2½ hours

1. We leave Keld by the same route we entered, at the bottom end of the village, along the waymarked Pennine Way footpath. We only stay on this for a couple of hundred yards though, until the path forks at a finger post.

2. We take the left branch, following the Pennine Way, but now downhill quite steeply on a rough path, through a pair of ancient stone gate posts and down to a footbridge.

3. The bridge crosses the Swale and on the other side we keep left, circling an open green space that could have been created specifically for summer picnics. The waterfalls of East Gill add a sense of drama to the location.

4. The rocky path bends right, climbing to meet another path, with a helpful finger post. A right turn would take us along Wainwright's Coast to Coast route, left is the Pennine Way and the Swale Way. Turn left, along what is now a raised track, climbing towards trees.

5. Views to the left open up dramatically as we climb this path; Keld is laid out before us and over our left shoulder is Kisdon Hill, part of the old Corpse Road to Grinton. After 100-150 yards we arrive at a gate which opens on to a farm yard with many path options.

6. Straight ahead is the Pennine Way up a grassy bank, but we're heading left now, around the back of the house on

a wide gravel track, flanked by a fine stone wall, to a metal vehicle gate (NY 89494 01254).

7. Go through the gate and follow the vehicle track as it contours the hillside. A wire fence on our left separates us from the wonderful view of Swaledale, what's left of it.

8. Over the next ½ a mile the track negotiates a couple more gates, passes old field barns and then bends down to cross Stonesdale Beck on a wide, rickety bridge.

9. Stay on the track for another 100 yards or so, through another wide gate, climbing now, up to another gate and the tarmac of Stonesdale Lane, which connects Swaledale to the legendary Inn at Tan Hill. Down to your left you may be able to see the unusual Yurts at Keld Bunk Barn.

10. Head uphill on the lane for just a few yards, looking out for a wide wooden gate on the other side of the road (NY 88613 01587). Go through this and follow the green path beside the dry stone wall on our right. The Swale is visible intermittently, through the trees down to our left.

11. The path climbs gently up to another gate and then undulates as it tries to contour the hillside, always with the fence, or a wall on our left and the open fell on our right. Conditions can be a bit muddy after rain, but the path is clear at all times.

We are now walking along the top of the limestone cliffs of Cotterby Scar. Below, the Swale suddenly drops about 5 feet, creating the popular waterfalls of Wain Wath Force.

---

12. Cross a ladder stile over a dry stone wall and continue beside the fence. Another couple of hundred yards and we cross a tiny footbridge and then another ladder stile. We lose the fence now, passing under trees and Low Bridge should become visible down to our left.

13. Go through a gap in the wall that appears to our front and follow the wall down to a four wheel drive track 100 yards further on (NY 87693 01624). Turn left onto this and drop down to meet the Swale at the bridge. A lime kiln sits beside the path here.

Lime kilns are scattered all over this limestone landscape. They produced huge quantities of lime to meet the needs of local landowners and farmers, who used it as fertilizer for their fields and in the mortar they needed for their building work.

The hollow main body of the kiln would be filled with repeating layers of crushed limestone and fuel; perhaps peat, wood or coal. Once filled, a fire was lit in the hollow at the bottom of the kiln and this ignited the fuel in the kiln, burning the limestone into more useful lime. Once cooled, the lime would be raked out of the hole in the base.

14. Cross the bridge, through the gate and turn right along the road. We only have to use the B6270 for ½ a mile, until we reach High Bridge. We don't cross this bridge though, instead, leave the tarmac, along a track, then through a wide metal gate (NY 87032 01326).

15. Beyond the gate, cross a narrow beck on wide stone slabs. Here the track continues into a field, used by Hoggarths campsite, but we bear left between the beck and the wall, up to a field barn.

The Swale at Hoggarths, looking downstream to High Bridge

16. Turn right in front of the barn, through a wooden gate and along a wide green track with the wall on our right. We

follow the wall for a couple of hundred yards until it ends and then we follow the Swale on our right.

17. It's still too early for lunch, but perhaps a short rest can be justified here. This is one of the last suitable places to sit and commune with the river we have followed for so long, we're less than a mile from the source now.

18. Continue with the river on our right, to a metal gate in a wall across our path (covered in white nylon sheeting at the time of writing). In the field beyond, head for the bridge across the river (NY 86437 01153). Cross this impressive old structure and turn sharp left along the opposite bank.

19. By following a fence on our left we reach a wooden gate which takes us into a rough pasture with the ivy-covered farmhouse at Firs, on the far side. Make your way across to this.

20. Just before the house we need to go through two wooden gates, the second of which has "Footpath" painted on it. Beyond the gates, our path runs along the grassy strip, to the left of the house, to another wide wooden gate.

21. Go through this and follow the green path across the field, passing beneath the power lines. The green path soon becomes a vehicle track, passing through a metal gate and after 100 yards or so, meets a more substantial gravel track (NY 85883 00989). We have a short out-and-back trip to visit the source and then we'll return here to continue.

The fine stone bridge you can see to the left - the first such structure the young Swale will flow beneath - and the one we crossed a few minutes ago were built in 1840 by the Alderson family, who lived in Stone House, the now empty farm we are about to walk past.

---

22. Turn left, through a wooden gate and follow the track, past Stone House for about 200 yards until we reach a ford in the river. This is Birkdale Beck, coming in from the right. If we turn left and follow this beck for a few yards you will see Great Sleddale Beck, coming down from the

hills ahead of us. Where these two becks meet, their confluence, is where the River Swale begins.

23. In theory, our walk finishes here, we've walked the Swale from its end to its source. However, unless you have a friend with a boat, or a helicopter, we need to walk out to civilisation before we can celebrate.

PART 2 - THE SOURCE OF THE SWALE TO NINE STANDARDS RIGG

Approx 5 miles (8 km) - 2½ to 3½ hours

1. Once you've paid your respects to the river, retrace your steps, past Stone House and back to the junction of paths. Beyond the wooden gate, continue along the obvious track as it climbs up towards the road.

2. We stay on the track for only about 250 yards. There's no obvious exit point, but as the road begins to bend right we need to keep straight on (NY 85653 01120), across the rough pasture, towards the house on the hillside ahead. There is a faint path through the grass, but you're just as likely to see the gap in the dry stone wall that runs across our path and the wooden stile we need to use.

3. In the next field the path is slightly more obvious, but not much. If in doubt, aim for a point between the house and the trees, where we will meet a rough vehicle track. Turn right onto this and climb up to a gate in the wall at the top of the farm drive (NY 85373 01304).

4. Beyond the gate, we keep hard left, beside the wall. Again, the path is vague at best, but all we're really doing is delaying the climb up to the road, which is to our right, hidden by the lie of the land. If we stick to the sheep trod beside the wall we'll soon meet a large white boulder; turn half right here and cut uphill, across the pasture, keeping to the right of the grassy lumps, to the road.

5. At the road you'll probably find a finger post (NY 85090 01401), which would have been useful earlier, and the entrance to the access track for Ellers. Strike out along the tarmac of the B6270, which is fairly quiet and has a narrow grass verge in places too.

The hills that form the skyline to the left are part of the Mallerstang Ridge. In the space of a few hundred yards along this ridge, rise the Rivers Ure and Eden, which head off in different directions in search of the sea. The source of Great Sleddale Beck can also be found here, so indirectly, the Swale too, is born from these peat hags.

Behind us is the impressive bulk of Great Shunner Fell, identifiable by the tiny dot of its summit shelter, visible even from this distance (providing it's not covered in cloud).

6. We follow the road for 1½ miles, through Birkdale now, rather than Swaledale, but it's still very pretty. You may be thinking about a lunch stop soon and there are plenty of sheltered spots beside the road to sit and take a break. This is not the case once we begin the ascent of Nine Standards Rigg though, so bear this in mind as you progress.

7. Just before we reach a dog-leg in the road, marked by a prominent road sign, look for a stony four wheel drive track leaving the road on our right (NY 83141 02694). Follow this track, as it twists and climbs, for about 400 yards until you see a finger post pointing onto the moor.

8. Turn left, off the track, onto a grassy path. We are now borrowing part of Wainwright's Coast to Coast (C2C) path to get us to Kirkby Stephen. This has a number of advantages that will become apparent over the course of the next couple of miles.

If you're walking outside of the months specified on the finger post don't worry. The C2C has seasonal alternative paths to help reduce the burden on the hill we are about to cross. Perhaps if the Swale Way becomes as popular we'll need to consider the same approach, but in the meantime, carry on.

9. The first advantage of using the C2C is that the path on the ground should be fairly easy to spot, at least for the first part of the ascent. If the weather is fine, you should also be able to see a tall pillar on the high point ahead of us. That's our first goal.

Section Six - Keld to Kirkby Stephen

10. If it's been raining a lot recently then you'll be crossing wet and soggy ground all along this path. Long legs will prove useful now as we step, lunge, jump and splash our way over the wet bits. About ¾ of a mile (and 250 feet of ascent) after leaving the four wheel drive track we will arrive at the pillar (NY 83103 03788). This is Millstone Pillar, a crafted cairn of tapering stones that serves as a great excuse to pause, admire the views and take a few photographs.

11. Beyond the pillar the path becomes a bit more vague, but keep heading uphill. Our next goal is almost exactly due north from here, but the path bends slightly to avoid boggy ground. Previous C2C walkers will have left footprints in the peat, so keep an eye out for these if you lose the path.

12. Shortly after leaving the pillar you should be able to see the pile of stones at Coldbergh Edge. If you delayed lunch, this is your final dry seat until Nine Standards (NY 82834 04377).

13. The path becomes faint again after we leave the stones and we enter the infamous peat hags of Nine Standards Rigg. A compass or a GPS will be useful, but if visibility is good, just keep heading uphill. It's about ¾ of a mile to the obvious high point of White Mossy Hill (NY 82899 05323), and from here the path is more obvious, but probably not drier.

If you manage to leave the Yorkshire Dales National Park without wet peat on your boots then you'll have done well. White Mossy Hill marks our exit from the park and a wide, perpetually boggy strip of peat delineates the boundary.

---

14. We're heading downhill now, for a short way, aiming for a finger post and the start of the slabs (NY 82728 05661) that have been laid over the worst of the peat hags; another benefit of using the C2C path. Opinion may be divided on their presence here, but they are used to protect the delicate peat bog; which, as we've seen, has taken something of a hammering from walkers over recent years.

15. A new boundary marker beside the path identifies the point where we leave Yorkshire and enter Cumbria. Keep left at the junction of slabs and imagine what crossing this next grough would be like without the slabs!

Pronounced "gruff" these natural channels in the peat moor can be extremely tricky to climb out of, especially when the peat is wet and the banks slide away under your feet.

16. The slabs don't last for long and we're quickly back on firm, rising ground, heading for our next target, the Ordnance Survey Triangulation Pillar (or trig point). This soon comes into view and along with it, the first sight of the Nine Standards themselves.

17. The trig point (NY 82542 06113) is a rather forlorn item, much beaten by weather, it has lost its metal benchmark, but still marks the high point of the hill, and indeed the walk itself at 662m (2,172 ft) above sea level. A short walk, via the commemorative hill finder, takes us to the cairns after which this hill is named.

The original purpose of the cairns is lost in time, but many theories abound; some outlandish and others quite prosaic. They are most likely just a boundary marker, between the old county of Westmorland and Swaledale. The abundance of building material explains how they could be built, but not why so many were needed and why they are so large. Some stood even taller, reaching up to 4m in the past.

The panorama from the cairns is incredible, with the Cross Fell range to the north, the Lakeland Fells to the north west, the Howgill Fells to the south west and of course Kirkby Stephen in the vale below us.

PART 3 - NINE STANDARDS RIGG TO KIRKBY STEPHEN

Approx 4 miles (6.5 km) - 1½ to 2 hours

1. After taking your fill of the scenery and the structures, head downhill, between two small cairns (NY 82462 06558) on a rough, badly eroded track. At least it's easy to follow. As you descend, the shapely profile of Wild Boar

Fell comes into view on the left, on the far side of the Eden Valley.

2. ½ a mile into the descent we cross a footbridge over Faraday Gill. The bridge could do with an extension as the gill seems to have widened since the bridge was installed.

3. Just beyond the bridge someone has built a slate seat beside the path, from which we could relax and admire the view - built for folk walking uphill rather than down, as all you probably want to do now is get into town.

4. ½ a mile beyond the bridge we meet a finger post (NY 81043 06742) and dry stone wall, both tell us to bear right and continue downhill. Now on a wide gravel track. A look back reveals the Standards on the hill. A look forward promises refreshments and journey's end.

5. The track is easy to follow, but hard on the feet after the bouncy turf (or sucking peat) of the hill and 1 mile after we joined it we reach a metal gate (NY 79924 07517). Go through this.

If you're heading directly for Kirkby Stephen station, rather than staying in the town tonight, then this is where you leave the Swale Way. Skip ahead to Part 4 on page 119 at this point.

6. If you're still reading then you're heading for the town, which is almost 2 miles from the station. Beyond the gate the path is flanked by gorse bushes, which add wonderful colour to the descent.

7. The track becomes a tarmac road now and other than some impressive views is fairly unremarkable and impossible to lose. We pass a cement quarry and factory before crossing a cattle grid and 1½ miles after joining the tarmac we reach the quarry entrance (NY 78473 08418).

Opposite, a wooden gate allows access to a viaduct, which once carried the South Durham and Lancashire Union Railway (1861-1962) on its descent from Stainmore.

8. Turn right, still going downhill into Hartley village.

9. A couple of hundred yards later, keep an eye out for a narrow bridge crossing the beck on our left (NY 78298 08633). It's marked by an old green metal finger post with faded lettering pointing us to Kirkby Stephen and Low Mill.

Hartley Fold House

10. Cross the bridge and turn left into the lane, then turn almost immediately right on a narrow path between walls, which brings us to a pair of gates and a tarmac path through a large field.

11. Follow the tarmac path for a couple of hundred yards, through a metal kissing gate and on to Frank's Bridge.

Frank's Bridge is a beautiful 17th century packhorse bridge and if you arrive into town early, is the perfect place to sit and finish whatever's left of your lunch. There is a coffin stone set into the grass here, part of another old Corpse Road. The building connected to the far side of the bridge is the town's old brewery; owned for a time by Francis (Frank) Birbeck.

12. Cross the bridge, continue straight ahead, up a flight of steps, turn right and then left and along a passage between shops, before emerging into the heart of the town.

13. Find the nearest place that serves the refreshment of your choice, sit down and pat yourself on the back. You've walked the length of one of Yorkshire's most iconic rivers and through its most beautiful dale.

If you fancy walking back, how about following the River Ure and Wensleydale? The Yoredale Way describes this walk and is available from the same author! **www.pocketroutes.co.uk**

KIRKBY STEPHEN

Kirkby Stephen is a great place to end, or start, a long distance path. It has plenty of amenities and is accustomed to supporting walkers, thanks to it being a popular stop on Wainwright's Coast to Coast walk.

The town is thought to have been first settled by the Vikings in the 10th century. By 1090 its name was recorded as "Cherkaby Stephen" and in 1353 it was granted a market charter by Edward III. The St. Luke's Fair charter is still celebrated in the town, each October.

The town has a branch of **Barclays Bank**, with an **ATM**, a **Post Office** and **Tourist Information**. There is a small **outdoor shop** which may be useful if you're planning on continuing along the Yoredale Way (**www.pocketroutes.co.uk**).

There are several pubs, including the **White Lion**, the **Black Bull** and the **Kings Arms**, the last two of which also provide **accommodation**. There are several excellent B&Bs in the town, including the **Jolly Farmers**, at the bottom end of town, towards the train station and **Fletcher House** and **Old Croft House** in the centre. **Kirkby Stephen Hostel** is not part of the YHA and may be hired as a whole, so check your dates in advance.

The pubs serve food, but there are other options as well, including an excellent **Chip Shop** which has both take-away and sit-in facilities and several other **tea rooms and cafés**.

A **Co-op mini supermarket** will provide all the groceries and packed lunch ingredients you could want, as well as snacks and cold drinks.

There are **public toilets** near the small market square, here also is a **bus stop** which will provide access to local towns. The **train station**, about 2 miles south of the town centre provides access to additional onward destinations.

sketched by Richard Collier

Kirkby Stephen signpost

PART 4 - LINK PATH TO KIRKBY STEPHEN STATION

Approx 3½ miles (6 km) - 1½ to 2 hours

1. Turn left after passing through the gate and follow the public footpath down the side of the hill to meet the track the leads to the buildings at Ladthwaite (NY 79624 06803).

2. Bear right away from the buildings, using the footpath through the trees and climb the side of the hill beyond.

3. The path soon descends, meeting the wall of a large enclosure (NY 78586 06384) before arriving at the tarmac of the B6270.

4. Turn right onto the road and follow it into the village of Nateby. Here we find the **Nateby Inn**. There are no refreshments at Kirkby Stephen station, so if you have time, it may be worth a pit stop here.

NATEBY

Nateby is a tiny village at the junction of the B6270 and B6259. It may offer an alternative overnight stop to the hustle and bustle to be found in Kirkby Stephen, but very little else is available here.

The only facility in the village is the **Nateby Inn pub** which provides accommodation, food and drink and also supports a small café, appropriately called the "**Walkers Tearoom**".

Nateby milestone

5. Walk down the right-hand side of the pub, through their beer garden and into the fields beyond (NY 77389 06759). Bear left across the fields, dropping down to cross a footbridge over the River Eden.

6. Climb up the next field to meet a farm track, along which we turn right. Follow this until you reach a house on the right and a cattle grid across the path. Turn left here (NY 77021 06441) and follow the path to the station.

The Swale Way

PART 3 - THE MAPS

"I was not able to light on any map or work giving the exact locality of the Castle Dracula, as there are no maps of this country as yet to compare with our own Ordnance Survey maps."

Jonathan Harker, from Bram Stoker's 'Dracula'

The maps for this walk are available electronically, direct from the website, at no extra charge. Simply use the password provided below to access the special location on the website.

From this page, you will be able to download the maps in PDF format. You can then print the maps and carry them separately from the book, perhaps to be placed in a waterproof map case.

It also ensures you have the latest versions of the maps, with any amendments that may have been made since the book was published.

Webpage: **bit.ly/swale-maps**

Password: **17te8XTa**

If you have any problems accessing or downloading the maps, please send an email to: **stuart@pocketroutes.co.uk**

OVERVIEW MAP

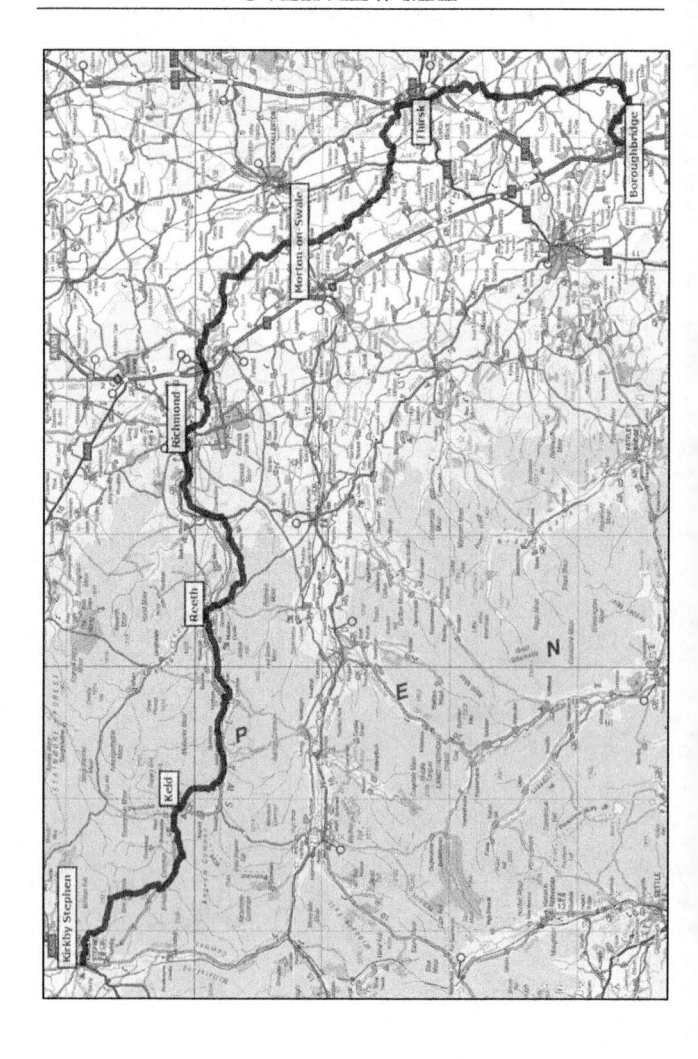

NOTES

Printed in Great Britain
by Amazon